THE TECHNIQUE AND PRACTICE OF LISTENING IN INTENSIVE PSYCHOTHERAPY

Also by Richard D. Chessick, M.D., Ph.D.

Agonie: Diary of a Twentieth Century Man

Intensive Psychotherapy of the Borderline Patient

Freud Teaches Psychotherapy

How Psychotherapy Heals

Why Psychotherapists Fail

The Technique and Practice of Intensive Psychotherapy

A Brief Introduction to the Genius of Nietzsche

Psychology of the Self and the Treatment of Narcissism

Great Ideas in Psychotherapy

What Constitutes the Patient in Psychotherapy

A Dictionary for Psychotherapists

THE TECHNIQUE AND PRACTICE OF LISTENING IN INTENSIVE PSYCHOTHERAPY

Richard D. Chessick, M.D., Ph.D.

JASON ARONSON INC.
Northvale, New Jersey
London

The author gratefully acknowledges permission to reprint excerpts from the following:

Notes upon a case of obsessional neurosis, by S. Freud (1909), *The Standard Edition of the Complete Psychological Works of Sigmund Freud*, vol. 10, copyright ©1955 by The Hogarth Press. Reprinted by permission of Sigmund Freud Copyrights Ltd., The Institute of Psycho-Analysis, and The Hogarth Press, London.

Catatonia, by K. L. Kahlbaum, copyright ©1973 by The Johns Hopkins University Press. Reprinted by permission of The Johns Hopkins University Press, Baltimore, MD.

Models of the mind and data-gathering in clinical works, by E. A. Schwaber, published in *Psychoanalytic Inquiry*, vol. 7, no. 2, copyright ©1987 by M. Bornstein, J. Lichtenberg, and D. Silver. Reprinted by permission of The Analytic Press, publisher, Hillsdale, NJ.

Returning to Freud: Clinical Psychoanalysis in the School of Lacan, by S. Schneiderman, copyright ©1980 by Yale University. Reprinted by permission of Yale University Press, publisher, New Haven, CT.

The two analyses of Mr. Z., by H. Kohut, published in *International Journal of Psycho-Analysis*, vol. 60, copyright ©1979 by Heinz Kohut. Reprinted by permission of *International Journal of Psycho-Analysis*, London.

Doing Psychotherapy, by M. F. Basch, copyright ©1980 by Basic Books, Inc. Reprinted by permission of Basic Books, Inc., New York.

The case of Ellen West: an anthropological-clinical study, by L. Binswanger, published in *Existence: A New Dimension in Psychiatry and Psychology*, edited by R. May, E. Angel, and H. F. Ellenberger, copyright ©1958 by Basic Books, Inc. Reprinted by permission of Basic Books, Inc., New York.

The Transference in Psychotherapy: Clinical Management, edited by E. Schwaber, copyright ©1985 by Evelyne Albrecht Schwaber, M.D. Reprinted by permission of International Universities Press, New York, publisher; E. Schwaber, editor; J. Arlow, author.

Attention and interpretation, by W. Bion, published in *Seven Servants*, copyright ©1970 by W. R. Bion, copyright ©1977 by Jason Aronson Inc. Reprinted by permission of Jason Aronson Inc., Northvale, NJ.

First Softcover Edition 1992

Library of Congress Cataloging-in-Publication Data

Chessick, Richard D., 1931–
The technique and practice of listening in intensive psychotherapy.
Includes bibliographies and index.
1. Psychotherapy. 1. Title. [DNLM: 1. Psychotherapy–methods. WM 420 C524ta]
RC480.5.C468 1989 616.89'14 89-104
ISBN 0-87668-862-8 (hardcover)
ISBN 0-87668-300-6 (softcover)

Manufactured in the United States of America. Jason Aronson Inc. offers books and cassettes. For information and catalog write to Jason Aronson Inc., 230 Livingston Street, Northvale, New Jersey 07647.

This book is dedicated to

my grandchildren. . . .

May their world be a better one.

συλλάψιες ὅλα καὶ οὐχ ὅλα,
συμφερόμενον διαφερόμενον,
συνᾶδον διᾶδον· ἐκ πάντων
ἓν καὶ ἐξ ἑνὸς πάντα.*

—Heraclitus (quoted by Aristotle,
De Mundo 5,396b20)

*Things taken together
are both whole and not whole,
adhering and flying apart,
singing in harmony,
incompatibly dissonant.
Out of all things
emerges a unity;
out of the one
comes all things.

(Translation by Dr. Chessick)

CONTENTS

ACKNOWLEDGMENTS

THIS WORK WOULD NOT have been possible without the consistent support and encouragement of a number of respected friends and colleagues over the past few years. I wish to especially thank Dr. Pramote Chaowasilp of Bangkok, Thailand, Dr. János Csorba of Budapest, Hungary, Dr. Ayoma Ojwana of Nairobi, Kenya, and Dr. Otto Dörr Zegers of Santiago, Chile, for their interest, their willingness to engage in dialectic with me, and their opening up new and alternative vistas. Dr. Stanley Lesse and my co-members of the editorial board of the *American Journal of Psychotherapy* have always been willing to consider and to publish preliminary communications that eventually became incorporated in this book, and I appreciate their help very much.

I am deeply grateful to the membership of the American Society of Psychoanalytic Physicians, and especially my friends and colleagues Dr. George Train of the New York chapter and Dr. Allan Schwartzberg of the Washington chapter, for their unflagging interest in my evolving work and for presenting me with the Sigmund Freud Award in 1989. Members of the Japanese Psychoanalytic Society and a number of other psychiatrists and psychologists who patiently attended our meeting in Tokyo and questioned me about some of the sections of this work have a special place in my heart; the organizers of that meeting at the Keio University School of Medicine Hospital in Tokyo were my friends and colleagues Dr. Osamu Kitayama and Dr. Keigo Okonogi, and I wish to thank them very much for this opportunity and for their hospitality to me while I was in Japan. The lengthy discussion that followed was only possible because of the invaluable help of the translator at the meeting, my daughter Ms. Linda Haydel, who also served as our charming guide and hostess.

Several sections of this manuscript were attentively listened to and discussed at the end of a long day by a large segment of the membership of the American Academy of Psychotherapists at their training institute and annual conference in 1988; I want to express my gratitude to them, and especially to Ms. Melissa Lawler, Chairperson of the planning committee, who worked diligently for two years to set up that meeting. Last but not least, I am deeply grateful to the members of my psychotherapy case seminar, friends and colleagues, who have for years now faithfully attended and actively participated in the sometimes fiery monthly meetings at my home and, because of their stimulation and support, have enabled me to improve and clarify my clinical work and teaching.

My administrative assistant, Ms. Elizabeth Grudzien, deserves praise and thanks for her loyal and indefatigable energy and help in the many tasks required to put together such a manuscript, and Ms. Wanda Sauerman typed and retyped the pages in her usual efficient and dependable manner.

INTRODUCTION

PSYCHOANALYTIC LISTENING is only partly a technique that can be learned; at its base it is an interpersonal art which, like any artistic endeavor, requires talent and sensitivity. This book is intended to facilitate the teaching and learning of psychoanalytic listening, but the therapist's prior development of interpersonal skills, appropriate sublimations, personal motivations, and other intrapsychic compromise formations are fundamental to the mastery of this complex and creative process.

The book consists of eight chapters. Drawing on the work of Freud and his followers, the first chapter introduces the problems encountered in attempting to develop an optimal technique and practice of listening in intensive psychotherapy. The complexity of the topic as it has evolved over this century is illustrated by a discussion of the "alternative mode" for psychoanalytic listening recently advocated by Schwaber.

The second chapter delineates basic approaches and principles selected from various authors whose work I have found especially useful in thirty years of clinical work in psychoanalytic psychotherapy. These principles are discussed at length in Chapter 2 and illustrated by my annotations of detailed case material in subsequent chapters. Each chapter supplies appropriate references for further reading and study of the clinical material.

The third chapter introduces the challenging but highly rewarding task of listening to the psychotic patient and contains my annotations of verbatim or semiverbatim reports from case material of Kraepelin, Kahlbaum, Binswanger, and Lacan.

The fourth chapter focuses on listening to the so-called borderline patient, and includes my annotations of verbatim or semiverbatim case material reported by Basch, Chessick, and others.

The fifth chapter deals with listening to the neurotic patient and presents my annotated report of Freud's first seven sessions with Paul Lorenz (the Rat Man).

The sixth chapter explores the subject of empathic understanding and listening to narcissistic patients and offers my annotations of detailed case material published by Kohut and his followers.

The seventh chapter focuses on listening to the notorious, "difficult" patient and presents my annotations of a detailed case presentation and discussion of this subject reported by Arlow.

The eighth chapter illustrates the dangers when the

therapist is *not* listening and discusses the difficulties involved in teaching psychoanalytic listening.

The best starting point for understanding the technique and practice of listening in intensive psychotherapy remains the famous papers on technique, written by Freud from 1911 to 1915. These will be reviewed in the first chapter. In this work, Freud (1912) presents his well-known basic formula for psychoanalytic listening:

> He must turn his own unconscious like a receptive organ towards the transmitting unconscious of the patient. He must adjust himself to the patient as a telephone receiver is adjusted to the transmitting microphone. Just as the receiver converts into sound waves the electric oscillations in the telephone line which were set up by sound waves, so the doctor's unconscious is able, from the derivatives of the unconscious which are communicated to him, to reconstruct that unconscious, which has determined the patient's free associations. [pp. 115–116]

Over the years since 1912, it has become apparent that matters are considerably more complicated than Freud thought. The nineteenth-century ideal of the neutral, objective scientist collecting data as a value-free, context-free, atheoretical receiving apparatus has been shown to be impossible. All data and data collection presuppose theories, values, and some sort of previously established ideology. The "telephone receiver" of today's therapist must, in my opinion, be able to be tuned to at least five data-organizing channels, either simultaneously or by oscillating from channel to channel, in order to achieve a complete understanding of the patient's material. The most useful channels, as demonstrated by my clinical experience, are the following:

1. Freud's drive/conflict/defense orientation—the classical psychoanalytic approach as delineated and illustrated,

for example, by Arlow (1985). This is always the primary and preferred mode of listening and is the initial stance for any form of psychoanalytically oriented investigation and treatment.

2. The object relations approach. Especially useful is the work of two of its originators, Melanie Klein and Wilfred Bion, her analysand. This approach constitutes what Greenberg and Mitchell (1983) call the "relational/structure model" and focuses on the formation of psychic structure as a consequence of the earliest object relations, rather than of the nonspecific need for drive discharge. Although the earlier formulations of such theories by Klein and Bion are more fanciful, they have the advantage of offering a more sharply delineated alternative to the drive/conflict/defense channel of psychoanalytic listening.

3. The "sociocultural approach," initiated by Hegel, Feuerbach, Marx, and Nietzsche in philosophy and carried into the field of psychoanalytic psychotherapy and psychiatry by such authors as Fromm, Sartre, Lacan, and Foucault. This approach attributes the formation of psychic structure primarily to cultural determinants and denies any universal or permanent human essence or nature. What we "hear," when tuned into this channel, is a reflection of the kind of relationships and cultural milieu that are implicitly built into the prevailing economic system and ideology. The cultural background practices forming the patient's self are manifested to the therapist either directly, in the speech of the patient, or indirectly, as they are mediated through the family as it forms the child's personality. Since the method used by psychotherapists such as Jaspers (1972), who are advocates of this approach is often called *phenomenology* (to be explained and

discussed in Chapter 2), it will hereafter be referred to as the phenomenological channel.

4. The fourth channel tunes in to the realm of the self, developed into a precise technical investigational procedure with a theoretical base by Kohut (1971, 1977, 1984), that I have previously described (1985a). An interesting alternative to Kohut's way of focus on the self, with controversial emendations and "improvements," has been presented by Gedo (1979, 1981, 1984, 1986). In considering this channel, it is also important to review an excellent early attempt by Gedo and Goldberg (1973) to connect this realm of the self with Freud's changing viewpoints. The psychology of the self, whether one follows Kohut, Gedo, or others, is very important in psychoanalytic listening; it is a most exciting and as yet incomplete field of exploration with vast potential. Silverman (1987) also uses this model as one of the four models in his "multimodel approach." His other three suggested models are the Freudian "drive defense model," the object relations model, and "Mahler's symbiosis/separation–individuation model" (p. 156).

5. The final channel, the interactive approach, focuses on countertransference or more generally, on the here-and-now factors in the treatment, emphasizing the role of the analyst's participation. For example, Thomä and Kächele (1985) contend that the analyst must always ask, "What am I doing that causes the patient to have this anxiety and provokes this resistance?" and "What do I do to contribute to overcoming this resistance?" Such authors stress the interactional aspects of the psychoanalytic or psychotherapeutic process throughout the therapy. Thomä and Kächele believe that their emphasis on the interactional aspects is much deeper than Sullivan's interpersonal theory, which, they say,

neglects intrapsychic factors and does not recognize that the analyst's participation constitutes significant intervention from the very beginning of treatment.

The literature is replete with arguments and counterarguments about which stance or which channel is best; these arguments vary from intense insistence that one and only one channel is the proper one—often with the implication that therapists tuned to other channels are in need of further analysis—to Kohut's (1984) rhetorical argument that it makes no fundamental difference which stance the therapist uses, so long as the patient recognizes an empathic response.

This book discusses the basic schisms among psychoanalytic theories best outlined by Greenberg and Mitchell (1983)—and the differing modes of listening that accompany them. As they portray it, the central contrast is between the drive/structure orientations and the relational/structure models; there are also so-called mixed-model strategies. Greenberg and Mitchell's book is fundamental to the study of our subject and will naturally lead us to examine the strategy of appropriate validation of our interventions and to consider how to listen to patients in such a way as to convince ourselves that we have heard them properly.

Bion's (1963, 1967) work, written in his unique rhetorical style and stressing the need to listen to the patient without memory, desire, or understanding, becomes especially significant in situations that confuse or stump us. Our only other recourse—and one that should be used more often than it is—is to seek consultation or supervision, or even to return to our own personal psychoanalysis. It will be repeatedly stressed that, regardless of orientation, *only the thoroughly psychoanalyzed therapist can listen properly and appropriately to the patient's material.* Any attempt to listen by an unanalyzed "therapist" will result in a collusion to disguise the basic problems and often results in a mutually destructive acting out (Chessick 1969a, 1971, 1974, 1977a, 1980a, 1985a).

A discussion of Bion (1963, 1967) would not be complete without a mention of his concept of the analyst's function as a container, or "toilet"—a significant aspect of psychoanalytic listening. The phenomenological approach (Atwood and Stolorow 1984) is especially useful in a study of this sort of interaction between patient and therapist. Similarly, we must consider Gill's (1982) thoughtful contribution on the influence of the analyst's here-and-now reality on the patient's transference, although many therapists are not in agreement with his controversial position on that subject.

Langs's (1978, 1982) descriptions of the various types of interpersonal fields are useful and appropriate, as are his warnings to listen carefully to all patient material for allusions to the therapist, even though his views tend to be rather extreme (Chessick 1982a).

The self psychologists, and especially Schwaber (1983a, 1986), have recently emphasized the importance of empathic listening, discussed at length elsewhere (Chessick 1985a). A more general and widely accepted version of this idea is found in Modell's (1976) concept of the therapeutic process as a "cocoon" which must be used for "holding" seriously disturbed patients so that they can comfortably communicate, at least in the early stages of treatment. Winnicott deserves the credit for making explicit this aspect of the technique and practice of psychoanalytic listening (Chessick 1977b).

Reik's (1954) early contribution of "listening with the third ear" stresses the intuitive art of psychoanalytic listening and helps us to determine, in any given case, to what extent such a holding or cocoon function is necessary before accurate transmission and listening can take place. At a deeper level, Wolf (1985) and Loewald (1986) stress the regressive aspects of the unique psychoanalytic listening situation on *both* the patient and the therapist, and discuss the consequences of this for possible distortions in the listening process. An excellent clue to such distortions is offered in Gabbard's (1982) focus on the "exit lines" of both the patient and the therapist at the end of each treatment session.

Special problems in the interactive disruption of psychoanalytic listening must be discussed; for example, how are we to manage the archaic transference (Gedo 1977, Gunther 1984) that threatens to destroy the treatment and requires an immediate and appropriate therapeutic response?

The therapist's basic maturity and human qualities, along with his or her thorough personal psychoanalysis, are the fundamental requirements for accurate judgments, successful psychoanalytic listening, and valid, "in-tune" responses. It is primarily these responses that demonstrate the therapist has indeed heard the patient properly, and that build a trusting relationship and propel the treatment forward. Papers by Greenson (1974), Lipton (1977a, 1979, 1983), and Stone (1981) will be reviewed as illustrations of these fundamental human qualities. However, the bulk of this book will be devoted to annotation of clinical material in order to demonstrate the application of my approach in daily work with patients.

ONE

BASIC PRINCIPLES

THE MOST FAMOUS DICTA from Freud on the subject of psychoanalytic listening are to be found in his (1912) paper "Recommendations to Physicians Practicing Psychoanalysis." Here, Freud, in rejecting any special expedient—even that of taking notes—suggests the basic principle for the technique of psychoanalytic listening:

> It consists simply in not directing one's notice to anything in particular and in maintaining the same "evenly suspended attention" in the face of all that one hears. [pp. 111–112]

EVENLY SUSPENDED ATTENTION

Freud's technique of listening with evenly suspended attention constitutes an effort to avoid prescinding from the patient's material, in order to prevent the therapist from making any selection out of preconceived expectations. He wishes to avoid the danger of the therapist's never discovering anything that he or she does not already know, and of distorting what is perceived to fit experience-distant theoretical preconceptions.

The question of whether the therapist really can give such equal notice to everything communicated by the patient has often been raised, but only recently has it been answered increasingly in the negative. Many experienced therapists have learned that everyone approaches the data provided by the patient's free associations and behavior during sessions with a certain mental set—one that is based on either conscious or preconscious theoretical and philosophical conceptions. This mental set determines what is perceived and what is selected, *regardless* of the therapist's effort to listen with evenly suspended attention (Goldberg 1987b). A stance of evenly suspended attention is a necessary, deliberately conscious effort to reduce the influence of this mental set. This stance is enhanced greatly if therapists are *aware* of how their preconceptions influence all aspects of their perception of the patient.

A typical example of how such preconceptions interfere is the insistence on taking full notes or tape recordings of a patient's material. Freud (1912) makes it a rule not to take such notes, although he concedes:

> No objection can be raised to making exceptions to this rule in the case of dates, the text of dreams, or particular noteworthy events which can easily be detached from their context and are suitable for independent use as instances. [p. 113]

In any other circumstances, the writing of notes ties up one's mental activity, as Freud says, in a way that "would be better employed in interpreting what one has heard"; in addition, it carries the danger of selection as one writes the notes. It is far preferable that notes be taken immediately after the session. Or, if one's memory is as prodigious as Freud's, one can take notes in the evening, after the day's sessions are over, as Freud did.

The use of tape recorders is fraught with even greater danger because the use of these machines *invariably* interferes in some fashion with the production of the patient's material itself; the use of tape recorders represents an unwarranted intrusion into patients' privacy and encourages their exhibitionism as well as their suspicion that their material is being used for purposes other than the therapy itself—which it usually is.

I agree with Freud that extensive note taking (or tape recording) during sessions interferes with appropriate psychoanalytic listening, and that this is true in every case, including those that are conducted for "research." As Freud (1912) said:

> Cases which are devoted from the first to scientific purposes and are treated accordingly suffer in their outcome; while the most successful cases are those in which one proceeds, as it were, without any purpose in view, allows oneself to be taken by surprise by any turn in them, and always meets them with an open mind, free from any presuppositions. [p. 114]

In this same paper, Freud also offers the famous telephone-receiver analogy, already quoted in the Preface to this book. He goes on to explain that "if the doctor is to be in a position to use his unconscious in this way as an instrument in the analysis," then he or she must have "undergone a psycho-analytic purification"; otherwise the inevitable and innumerable "complexes of his own" disqualify the therapist from practicing intensive psychotherapy. Freud continues:

> There can be no reasonable doubt about the disqualifying effect of such defects in the doctor; every unresolved repression in him constitutes what has been aptly described by Stekel as a "blind spot" in his analytic perception. [p. 116]

DETECTING THE TRANSFERENCE

If we continue to follow Freud's papers on technique, we note that he (1913) explains how patients sometimes divide the treatment in their own way into an "official" portion on the couch and an informal, "friendly" portion upon leaving each session; they would like to pretend that the latter portion is not part of the treatment (p. 139). This material—produced before patients use the couch and as they leave—often gives a clue to the nature of the transference. Freud leads us from this discussion to his crucial point:

> *So long as the patient's communications and ideas run on without any obstruction, the theme of transference should be left untouched.* One must wait until the transference, which is the most delicate of all procedures, has become a resistance. [p. 139]

It is clear from Freud's writing that an important focus of psychoanalytic listening—if one includes both verbal and nonverbal communication—is to become aware, as sensitively and as quickly as possible, of the nuances of the development of transference. As Freud repeatedly remarks, the success or failure of a psychoanalytic therapy rests primarily on the identification and management of transference phenomena.

Thus, in the process of psychoanalytic listening, Freud (1914a) suggests that the therapist not attempt, at least at the beginning of the treatment, to focus on any particular moment or problem:

> He contents himself with studying whatever is present for the time being on the surface of the patient's mind, and he employs the art of interpretation mainly for the purpose of recognizing the resistances which appear there, and making them conscious to the patient. [p. 147]

EXPRESSION IN ACTIONS AND ALLUSIONS

One of the most difficult resistances to deal with in intensive psychotherapy and psychoanalysis, as Freud (1914a) goes on to point out in his magnificent paper "Remembering, Repeating, and Working-Through," occurs when the patient, instead of remembering what has been repressed, acts it out either within or outside of the analytic situation. As Freud says, "He reproduces it not as a memory but as an action; he *repeats* it, without, of course, knowing that he is repeating it" (p. 150). This is a common way in which patients "remember" previous relationships, and it is the task of the therapist, by careful listening, to become aware of what is being repeated in the course of the treatment, either in the relationship with the therapist or in the development of relationships with others outside of the treatment.

Thus the therapist must listen carefully to the patient's descriptions of current relationships for allusions to the relationship with the therapist, and for the repetition or displacement of disavowed aspects of this relationship outside of the consulting room. Later, we will discuss the question of whether this relationship represents a transference that is stirred up by childhood wishes, fantasies, and memories being reenacted in the relationship with the therapist or therapist substitutes, or whether it is predominantly a reaction to the here-and-now interaction between the patient and the therapist.

INTERFERING FACTORS

In his masterpiece "Observations on Transference-Love," Freud (1915) goes on to note that the analytic psychotherapist has "a three-fold battle to wage" (p. 170). The first of the forces that oppose the therapist are those in the therapist's own mind, "which seek to drag him down from the analytic level" (p. 170); today we would call this countertransference and the impulses to countertransference enactment. The second group of opposing forces come from outside the treatment. Patients are constantly assailed by relatives or friends and by "authorities" who are opponents of psychoanalysis; all of these individuals question the therapist's veracity, dispute the importance and value of the process, and repeatedly warn the patient not to get involved in it. The final set of opposing forces come from"inside" the analysis—that is, from the patients themselves. They may at first resist the appearance of their own emotionally charged material, such as that with sexual content, and may then experience the breaking forth of powerful desires, as in the archaic transferences, for example, which results in efforts to convert the therapist into an archaic selfobject or an object for the massive discharge of instinctual drives. These disruptive forces combine to make it difficult for the therapist to listen patiently and with evenly suspended attention, and they are all active all the time in every therapy.

The profound importance of Freud's discussion in these papers on technique has been recognized by Malcolm (1987). She deplores the literary establishment's unfortunate tendency to use Freud's case histories as examples of rhetoric and to present them as the heart of Freud's analytic work. As Malcolm correctly points out, the essence of Freud's mature clinical approach is contained in the papers on technique. She continues:

> It is in the particular, idiosyncratic, ineffable encounter between patient and analyst that the "story" of an analysis is lodged. The Rat Man's transferential wanderings around the consultation room and Freud's countertransferential "dry" manner with Dora are what constitute the "plot" of an analysis, and it is in his papers on technique . . . that Freud codifies the clinical theory he has hitherto scattered piecemeal through his writings. [p. 100]

As we study the various transcripts of patient–therapist interchanges in this book, we will learn how the three groups of forces that Freud named continually interfere with the therapist's effort to achieve effective psychoanalytic listening. The conscientious psychoanalytically oriented therapist's untiring effort to listen effectively constitutes the first part of the core of all good psychoanalytically oriented work because it leades to understanding. (The second part, interpretation, is not covered in detail in this book.) Proper interpretation or communication of this understanding deepens and solidifies the patient's self-understanding and enhances the patient's subsequent capacity to put this understanding to use in changing the very fabric of his or her character and in altering an unfavorable life situation. All such change is predicated, however, on the first step: proper psychoanalytic listening.

LISTENING WITH THE THIRD EAR

These suggestions from Freud were carried to an intuitive extreme in a book by Reik (1954), which unfortunately, has faded into obscurity. According to Reik, the analyst perceives the patient's unconscious mind by using his or her own unconscious as a sense organ—not by reasoning or by applying theoretical rules: "The psychoanalyst has to learn how one mind speaks to another beyond words and in silence" (p. 144).

The analyst's capacity for unconscious perception becomes crucial, and Reik refers to the organ for this perception—borrowing from Nietzsche's (1968) *Beyond Good and Evil*—as "the third ear" (p. 144). Reik states:

> We can best compare the psychical process with the act of vision, in which a stimulus is transmitted to the brain by the optic nerve, and every ray of light is projected again into the external world. The other person's impulse, which has unconsciously roused a corresponding impulse in the observer, is seen externally like the image on the retina. The observation of other people's suppressed and repressed impulses is only possible by the roundabout way of inner perception. In order to comprehend the unconscious of another person, we must, at least for a moment, change ourselves into and become that person. We only comprehend the spirit whom we resemble. [p. 361]

Reik addresses Fenichel's criticism that he goes too far toward the extreme of making too little use of reflective reason. He insists that his technique is indeed systematic and does not violate Fenichel's dictum (1) that psychoanalysis must lead from the poetic or intuitive grasp of the unconscious to a natural science of the human soul, and (2) that it must lead to ranging analytic technique within the rational categories:

> We all regard reason as the supreme authority in scientific research. In the actual course of research conscious and unconscious processes of thought will cooperate in variable proportions to reach our result. In the field of analytic technique this ration of conscious intellectual effort to unconscious comprehension of the psychical material will be special and peculiar. An analyst's real instrument is his own unconscious, which has to seize upon the patient's unconscious processes, "intuitively," as is incorrectly said. [p. 388]

For Reik, intuition—"the analytic technique of cognition of unconscious processes"—represents "oscillation between the conscious and unconscious labors of the intellect and imagination" (p. 389). Reik contends that the employment of the unconscious as a vital organ of apprehension is the special peculiarity of the analytic method and is the characteristic that differentiates the analytic method from other scientific methods. He maintains that the application of conscious and rational thought in analytic investigation is common to all scientific methods and goes beyond listening with the third ear into testing and verifying the ideas that arise from the unconscious, in linking them with previous knowledge, in drawing certain conclusions, in criticizing them, and, generally, in rigorously examining the psychological data. Reik argues that conscious knowledge and reason have not the first but the last word in the process of analytic discovery; what is crucial and particular to the psychoanalytic method is the gathering of data by listening with the third ear.

CHOICE OF THEORY

Since Freud's time, increasing attention has been paid in all fields of science to the effect of the observer's theoretical preconceptions and activities on clinical data. This leads to the question of the choice of theory, which has remained an unresolved controversy in the analytic literature. For example, Goldberg (1987a) wonders if failure to learn the theory and practice of self psychology might be a product of the countertransference of a traditional analyst. This type of explanation has been generalized in analytic controversy, as cleverly described by Shane (1987):

> It is well known to those who do not hold that particular theory that, for example, all Kleinians are crazy and full of rage, all self psychologists cover their fear of aggression with the syrup of empathy, all classical analysts mask their fear of the primitive with a rigid insistence on mature responsibility, and all developmentalists dignify the banalities of the nursery out of a timid need to avoid oedipal passions. Moreover, all of these can agree on one proposition; the mixed-model theorists are either obsessively, phobically, or stupidly incapable of commitment, and, confusing apples with oranges, end up with a sloppy, inelegant fruit salad. [p. 201]

So we are confronted with an impossible and paradoxical set of *ad hominem* interpretations condemning both those who adhere to one theoretical model and those who attempt to apply a mixture of models! Our situation is not entirely hopeless, however, for, as Shane adds, "it is remarkable how each framework does seem to add something to our understanding of a given patient, even where the contributions among theories are incompatible" (p. 201).

This important statement addes credence to our attempt

to view the proper stance for psychoanalytic listening and the understanding of the data thus obtained, from a variety of frameworks. Such a variety does not imply any negation of the psychoanalytic approach because, as Shane points out, there can still be a common psychoanalytic conceptual base. This base is manifest in that all psychoanalytic theories or frameworks deal with transference and countertransference issues, and all emphasize the crucial significance of infantile and childhood experience, the existence of a dynamic unconscious, the importance of free association, the crucial role of the Oedipus complex, the centrality of early selfobjects, and the primary role of the analyst and of analytic interpretation.

AWARENESS OF THEORETICAL PERSPECTIVES

The analyst's primary role has increasingly come into focus in the literature, especially in a series of papers by Schwaber (1981a,b, 1983a,b,c, 1985, 1986, 1987). Schwaber (1987) raises the crucial question about any framework or model:

> If the model determines how the material is understood and what is to be interpreted, is it not then assigned a primacy that goes beyond serving its purported function of organizing the data and broadening our perceptual scope? Is it not then given a use by which the analyst may render judgment about what is relevant, what is real, and what may be omitted in the patient's experience? Superimposed upon the clinical data, the model may supersede it, leaving unresolvable the debate about which theory best explains the data. [p. 262]

As an example, Schwaber (1987) quotes some of Mason's use of the Kleinian model as the basis for his extensive speculation, which she sees as inherent in Mason's following interpretation:

> The smallness of your penis and money also make you attack daddy's penis to make it bad and dangerous so that mommy hates it too. This causes men's sex today to frighten and disgust you because you still believe your little girl's view of it. You also get mad at me today because I am the "big father-analyst" and you are "only the little girl patient." You make my analysis bad and hurtful and it becomes "incomprehensible" and you can't take it in. [pp. 271–272]

Schwaber points out that these ideas are inferentially based and imply in this instance that the patient's experience in the transference is devoid of her perception of the analyst's responses to her. The analyst is telling the patient how the patient feels. He should be seeking to learn from *her*, and he should be "facilitating the patient's self-observing capacity by pursuing with her the moment-to-moment verbal and affective shifts" (p. 272).

Schwaber asks whether it is ever possible to forego our model as we listen and gather data, and whether we can ever manage to avoid contaminating clinical material with our own theoretical persuasions. If models are used to organize what we see and to expand the range of what we perceive, they can enrich our field of inquiry. But Schwaber (1987) insists that *awareness* of our chosen perspective may point to a discrepancy between our views and the patient's view of the same occurrence:

> Modern science teaches us that the observer's participation is an essential and fascinating element of the data. I make no argument for an atheoretical orientation, even if that were possible. I argue, rather, for our recognition that no matter what theory we

> espouse, we run the risk of using it to foreclose rather than to continue inquiry, to provide an answer rather than to raise a new question. I speak for a search for ways to sharpen our attunement to hear new cues from the patient that may tell us that we have, even if unwittingly, superimposed our view and used our theory to justify it. [p. 274]

The way of sharpening our attunement to the patient that I propose is to approach the data of psychoanalytic communication in this book from five more or less psychoanalytic models in turn, without definitively assigning preeminence to any one model in a given clinical situation, until after we have been open to examining the data in detail from five points of view. Without this approach, no material can be convincingly understood as falling under the rubric of a given model.

In addition, clinical experience unfailingly demonstrates two principles. The *first* of these is that a psychoanalytic model is the *only* acceptable one if we want to thoroughly and deeply understand our patients. Every psychoanalytic model, as explained previously, has more or less the same conceptual base, the dynamic unconscious, although they differ from each other in fundamental ways. All deal with transference and countertransference and use the method of free association. All view infantile and childhood experiences as crucial and stress preoedipal and oedipal factors to one degree or another. All in various ways and to different degrees emphasize repetition, the role of the analyst, and the importance of interpretation.

The *second* principle is that one neglects Freud's drive/conflict/defense orientation at one's peril. Many "alternative" approaches have been devised over the years to avoid both Freud's emphasis on sexuality and aggression as constituting the infantile core of the adult, and his central focus on the

Oedipus complex. As Lacan said, psychoanalysis has to be rediscovered over and over again. Many cases flounder when alternative stances are used for defensive purposes. This is a frequent cause of the need for reanalysis or for psychoanalysis after a "completed" psychotherapy. To avoid this common and very unfortunate pitfall, the primary model in approaching any patient material should be Freud's "drive/ structure" model (Greenberg and Mitchell 1983), and Freud's dicta for psychoanalytic listening as described at the beginning of this chapter should be followed whenever possible. Any departure from this channel should be tentative, and the possibility of defensive collusion should always be kept in mind.

Schwaber does not specifically advocate this procedure, but she does maintain (and I agree) that these models are neither interchangeable nor matters of personal preference. She explains:

> We must seek that model which best explains the data and best expands our perceptual field. Augmenting the focus on moment-to-moment verbal and affective cues, and on their possible connection to how the patient perceives our participation—silent or stated—may serve to narrow the leaps of inference we must make, facilitate the patient's capacity for self-observation, while simultaneously bring to light a further range of experiential and defensive phenomena. [Schwaber 1987, p. 275]

Surely Schwaber's attitude will help us toward our choice of a model, but in the process of psychoanalytic listening this choice is only valid for a given collection of the clinical data of psychoanalytic listening at any given time. There is no implication that a particular model will serve us in *all* situations. This fact—which so frustrates those who yearn for a single, universal system—has also been pointed out by Gedo and

Goldberg (1973), who actually offer a variety of models of the mind, all taken from or which they believe are consistent with traditional psychoanalytic theory; they attempt to show how different models are best applied to certain types of psychoanalytic data.

Schwaber's Approach

Although we have already reveiwed Schwaber's perspectives and conclusions, her views are so timely, important, and complementary (although not identical) to my own that we ought to examine them in greater detail. Schwaber (1985) develops her approach extensively, basing it on Freud's "monumental shift" (p. 173) from the seduction to the fantasy theory of neurosogenesis; this shift marked a critical turning point in the history of psychoanalysis and placed psychic reality as its decisive clinical domain. Freud's shift, says Schwaber, is based on the twentieth-century recognition that "reality" cannot be absolutely knowable; its assessment is a psychic function that therefore must contain within it the presence of the observer. Schwaber calls this "the reflection in depth psychology of the scientific revolution of our century, the era of relativity" (p. 173).

Schwaber insists that we recognize that at all times, and even unknowingly, we participate in the patient's experience; this participation, which may feel quite different to us than to our patients, tends to repeatedly escape our notice. She concludes that unless we are aware of this participation, we cannot remain attuned to the patient's material. For Schwaber, this means renouncing the possibility that we can be the final arbiter of what is reality, as distinguished from, for example, transference distortion. She adds, "Different theoretical models may change the options as to what and whether to interpret, but the overall clinical stance is influenced less by the choice of model than by the therapist's outlook on reality" (p. 175).

In earlier papers, Schwaber (1983a) elaborates on what she considers to be two alternative modes of psychoanalytic listening. In the "traditional" mode:

> As the experiential specificity of the analyst's contribution is not elaborated as intrinsic to the episode, implicitly then the analyst stands "outside," utilizing his own measure of "objective" reality, observing and interpreting the inner reality of the patient. [p. 521]

In Schwaber's (1983b) "alternative" mode, she attempts to understand the material at the moment it appears and in the context of the participation with the analyst:

> The objective of such close attunement to the analytic moment is to serve not as an interactive experience in its own right, but as an avenue for deeper recognition of the patient's intrapsychic world and thus as a pathway for reconstruction. [pp. 290–291]

This is not to imply that analysts can use this mode of attunement to forestall the occurrence of material or symptoms, or even that this should be their aim. Note how Schwaber differs from Kohut (1984), who *would* consider such close attunement a crucial therapeutic experience in its own right.

Shift in Perspective

Schwaber attempts to elaborate just how an intervention of the analyst is experienced perceptually and becomes a part of the totality of the patient's psychic state. She (1983a,c) calls this a shift in perspective, from the vantage point of the analyst's reality to one in which the organization of intrapsychic experience is the property of an inclusive system that includes the participation of the analyst. As she points out, this shift in perspective has considerable impact on the gathering of psychoanalytic data:

> Listening from within the patient's experience, weaving the perception of the analyst's contribution, silent or stated, into the elucidation of the subsequently emerging material, assigns different meaning to our understanding of transference, resistance, and memory—a relativity continually shifting, though with inherent continuity. [1983a, p. 522]

Transference under this approach is no longer thought of as a distortion, because this would imply that the analyst's view of reality is more correct than the patient's psychic view of the analyst, and that the analyst as an "outside" observer who "knows" reality could ascertain that distortion. This extreme approach sharply distinguishes Schwaber's alternative mode of analytic listening from the traditional mode. From her point of view, psychic experience is not separable from its context, and the transference is not separable from the real; there is not, as in the traditional view, a perspective from a hierarchy of realities—the more objective reality of the analyst as distinguished from the psychic reality of the patient.

Schwaber's (1983a) method is to maintain what she calls a "vigilant focus" (p. 531) on such nonverbal cues as shifts in the patient's affect or state in response to the analyst's interventions. The mode of attunement required to maintain this focus Schwaber (1981a) calls "empathy," which "requires some resonance of essential human alikeness with the experiential and perceptual world of our patients" (p. 382). Note the similarity of this conception to some of Reik's views, described previously.

In a more formal paper, Schwaber (1983c) differentiates between listening by sifting the material (1) from the vantage point of the analyst's reality in trying to aid the patient's observing ego in recognizing the distortions in his or her perceptions, and (2) from a focus from within the patient's perspective—that is, "to see in it a certain plausibility, however outlandish" (p. 379). This differentiation leads to a shift in the understanding of resistance, from a phenomenon arising from internal pressures within the patient, which the analyst as a blank screen can stand apart and observe, to that "in which the specificity of the analyst's contribution was seen as intrinsic to its very nature" (p. 381).

Such a shift requires clinical material that relates to the specific details of the analyst's participation—difficult to find in the psychoanalytic literature. As Schwaber points out, the patient's material is usually described in an already dynamically formulated fashion, and the reader is deprived of the opportunity to learn precisely what the analyst did or did not say. This condensed and already formulated report usually implies an assumption that the analyst is functioning effectively, with minimal countertransference experience, and that the specificity of his or her participation is therefore not germane to our understanding of the data.

Schwaber (1983c) gives several examples to illustrate the inaccuracy of this assumption. She claims that such an assumption is based on analysts' resistance to facing the centrality of their own unwitting participation in the patient's experience and also, upon Schwaber's self-reflection, on a resistance based on "the lack of concurrence with my own experience of myself" (p. 389). The latter may have deeper significance in that it resists our acknowledging that the truth we believe about ourselves "is no more (though no less) 'real' than the patient's view of us—that all that we can 'know' of ourselves is our own psychic reality" (p. 389).

PLACING SCHWABER'S VIEWS IN THE PRESENT APPROACH

There is no question that, complementary to Freud's technique, we must sharpen the focus on the impact of our contribution to the patient's experience. However, when we go to the extreme advocated by Schwaber, we are indeed introducing an alternative mode of psychoanalytic listening from that of Freud. Schwaber's clinical examples are instructive and persuasive, but they can easily lead to a relativism or even a nihilism in the employment of theoretical models—a stance that in itself could make a negative contribution to the patient's material. Therefore, in this book, I have relegated Schwaber's point of view as belonging to only one of the five models of theoretical understanding that must be used in a comprehensive listening process. I have sublated it under the self-psychological stance, although it is more extreme. Her underlying shift of outlook is one of several indispensable shifts in perspective, framework, stance, model, or channel of attunement that the experienced therapist should be able to make in examining clinical material. Furthermore, it is *the specific material itself* that should lead the therapist to apply any given model at any given time. This is not to insist on obsessively examining every bit of psychoanalytic data from the point of view of five models in turn. Patients lead us, at any given time, to the model that most appropriately fits the material they are presenting.

Admittedly, this approach is quite unsatisfactory to those who need or insist on one basic model on which to base their understanding, or one mode of attunement to the patient to use throughout the treatment. Unfortunately, although there are brilliant efforts to support the traditional Freudian model (Rangell 1988), there simply is not sufficient agreement in the field to allow us to make such a definitive choice. As discussed previously, both making this choice as well as refusing to choose one mode of attunement can be attacked on *ad hominem* grounds. Thus, this book approaches the problem as essentially unresolved and simply presents one clinician's current practical point of view. This leaves the suggestions contained herein regarding the practice and technique of psychoanalytic listening open to contradiction by the clinical experience of others and to the usual *ad hominem* deprecations.

Schwaber's (1986) admonition should be kept in mind by proponents of other models:

> The patient misjudges, misapprehends, and distorts, and it is the analyst who, even if silently, is making that judgment. It is precisely the *implicit* presence of such a hierarchical view that I wish to illustrate. Though we may all agree that it is "psychical" and not "material" reality that is our domain (Freud 1917), that we do not concern ourselves with absolute or "objective" truth, this position, even where it has been defended, on theoretical grounds, has not found its place in clinical application. [pp. 920–921]

Her insistence on sharpening our attunement to clinical moments—represented by a shift in affect or state, a turn of phrase, the transient appearance of a symptom or old behavior—and her advice that we "consider our participation, as the patient has perceived it *and as a central element in the transference*" (p. 929), facilitates the emergence of a deepening realm of psychic experience and adds an important dimension to our understanding of the patient. It is only on the basis of such thorough understanding that constructions and reconstructions in analysis can have a personal meaning for the patient and not be heard as an intellectual exercise or an abstract lecture coming from a distant and detached "authority."

VALIDATION

It is important to remember, as even Reik pointed out, that the understanding of the patient that we gain from these various channels for psychoanalytic listening is then to be translated into rational interventions. If we listen carefully, the patient's response to our interventions may serve as validation or negation of the accuracy of our understanding. Thus we are not engaging in a simply intuitive or "empathic" process without the possibility of at least quasi-empirical validation, as one might find in speculative philosophy, which later often depends on pure reason alone, or solely on "intuition." We are advocating a specific, carefully considered technique, a "praxis" (Ricoeur 1970) invented by Freud, in which patients lead us by their communications to our choice of models of understanding and then validate or negate the application of a given model within the data of each subsequent psychoanalytic session. These validating data are generated by the patient's response to interpretations based on our "understanding."

Thomä and Kächele (1985) correctly regard the patient's response to interpretations as "decisive": for examples they review Isaacs's (1939) catalogue of confirmatory responses. The patient may give verbal assent and cooperatively elaborate or produce further associations or memories. But even repudiation may be presented so as to provide a confirmation, accompanied, for example, by guilt, terror, or change of associations that could only occur if the interpretation was correct. The patient might suddenly remember a dream or bring one in the next day that is consistent with or elaborates on the interpretation; in a similar fashion, either memories or references to external situations may fall into place. Or, the patient may bring in corroborating information from relatives or friends. Most important is our careful attention to what happens in the transference. There may be an obvious resolution of anxiety and a shift in the transference such that, for example, the therapist changes from a dangerous figure to a helpful one.

All of this leads to a concept that is central to the thesis of Thomä and Kächele but beyond the scope of this book—Loewald's (1960) concept of the curative effect of the therapist as a new significant object in the patient's mental life *pari passu* with the development of insight. Thus one soon discovers that each proposed channel of psychoanalytic listening carries an implicit stance about psychological development, a view of psychic change, and assumptions about the curative factors in intensive psychotherapy. These stances contradict each other in fundamental ways, and they cannot at present be reconciled because they reflect profound disagreement about the nature of humans and the nature of knowledge itself. This is the postmodern condition, in which human being itself is under erasure, the world of Heidegger and Derrida.

TWO

LISTENING STANCES

WHAT ARE THESE FIVE standpoints or channels (models, perspectives, or frameworks) from which I propose we should tune in to the transmission from our patients? Each is based on premises about psychological development that are currently conflicting and irreconcilable.

1. The first model was presented by Freud and focuses on the Oedipus complex and the inevitable emergence, in a properly conducted psychoanalysis, of the need for drive satisfaction in the transference. This enables us to study the patient's infantile conflict and its subsequent vicissitudes in terms of defenses against the instinctual drives and the resulting crucial compromise formations produced by the ego in

dealing with its three harsh masters—the superego, the id, and external reality. Freud's structural theory, with the Oedipus complex as the focus, was developed for this purpose. At the core of it are the patient's childhood or infantile fantasies, derivatives of which repeat themselves over and over in the patient's mental life and behavior (Arlow 1985). We carefully listen for the derivatives of these fantasies and look for their reenactment in the transference. As previously stated, I believe that Freud's principles are the primary model, the starting point for all psychoanalytic listening and fundamental to all aspects of psychotherapy.

The *drive/conflict/defense orientation* of Freud, as it has been expanded and elegantly developed by traditional psychoanalysts, is usually sufficient for those forms of mental illness that have developed in individuals with a cohesive sense of self, relatively good ego functioning, and a sense of personal identity. These are mostly the disorders having an unresolved Oedipus complex at their center, in which pathological compromise formations have developed in an unsuccessful effort to deal with this nuclear oedipal problem. These formations, as they manifest themselves in symptoms and in maladaptive behavior, combine drive derivatives, depressive affect, ego defences, and superego functioning. The result, as Brenner (1982) describes it is "any combination of the following features: restriction of gratification of drive derivatives, too much anxiety or depressive affect, too much inhibition of functional capacity, too great a tendency to injure or destroy oneself, or too great a conflict with one's environment" (p. 161).

It is the widening scope of psychoanalytic psychotherapy that has forced us to employ the other channels, since many of our patients suffer from preoedipal deficits and lack the most primitive adaptive skills. Those who employ only the drive/conflict/defense orientation usually conceive of these problems as regressive, rather than as manifestations of structural deficit, and this is a central issue of disagreement. The questions of (1) whether such patients need more than interpretation and must be supplied with some sort of interpersonal experience with the therapist that is corrective or integrating, or even with education in adaptive skills, and (2) whether these patients are "beyond interpretation" and if not, to what extent they can respond to interpretations, remain hotly debated. These are the patients who have generated new approaches and new standpoints for psychoanalytic listening, challenging the skills and intuitive capacities of the psychotherapist and psychoanalyst.

2. The second channel uses the perspective of so-called *object relations theory* for its model. The work of M. Klein and her analysand Bion focuses on the patient's earliest projective and introjective fantasies as their derivatives appear in the object relatedness manifest in the transference and in the process of projective identification as it occurs in the analytic process. Bion (1963, 1967) emphasizes the "toilet function" of the analyst, whereby the analyst receives, metabolizes, and gives back in acceptable form the patient's unacceptable fantasies, affects, and expressions. This function is of enormous importance, especially in the treatment of borderline patients (Waldinger 1987), and it may be necessary for long periods in the early stages of treatment of such patients (Chessick 1982b).

Bion's concept of psychoanalytic listening is mystical but fascinating. He recommends a stance of abstaining from expectations, memory, desire, and understanding, leaving one simply open in faith. The basic belief is that, assuming the proper receptive stance, the patient will in each session transmit into the mind of the therapist what is needed for understanding. Eigen (1985) claims that Bion aims at the emotional truth of a session and obscurely describes this approach as "both Kantian and mystical," an attitude of pure receptiveness, leaving the therapist with nothing to hang on to, in an uncomfortable open state. As Eigen describes it, "One must tolerate fragmentation, whirls of bits and pieces of meaning and meaninglessness, chaotic blankness, dry periods and psychic dust storms" (pp. 326–327). Bion's advocacy, he seems to suggest, is for a trancelike, almost hallucinatory waiting or receptiveness. This extreme view seems to form some sort of link between Western and Eastern thought, which has not been generally accepted.

Klein (1975) developed the concept of projective identification (defined differently by every author), at the basis of which patients are thought to place into the analyst whatever self or object representations they wish to place there, leading to more therapeutic focus on preoedipal fantasies and processes. Klein inconsistently conceived of projective identification as a forceful, aggressive evacuation in fantasy consisting of a penetration into the object and a reinternalization of the object that was injured, which may lead to depression; or a reinternalization of the object that was rendered hostile, which may lead to persecutory hypochondria. She also described it as a very primitive means of communication leading to a "beyond the countertransference" distress in the therapist. So for Klein (Money-Kryle 1974) projective identification was also an interactional process, and hence there is an inconsistency in her concept.

Kernberg (1975, 1976, 1980) views projective identification as solely intrapsychic; for him it represents an incomplete projection. He presents three case illustrations of projection and projective identification that are worthy of serious study

(Kernberg 1987). In projection there is first the repressing of the intolerable, then projecting it onto the object, and finally "separating or distancing oneself from the object to fortify the defensive effort" (p. 796). In projective identification, which Kernberg views as more primitive, there is a similar projection of the intolerable onto the object, but the patient maintains a relationship with the object, now experienced as what has been projected, and "tries to control the object in a continuing effort to defend against the intolerable experience, and, unconsciously, in an actual interaction with the object, leads the object to experience what has been projected onto him" (p. 796).

A study of projective identification operating in the therapeutic process emphasizes the patient's earliest internalized object relations and yields data about how the patient as an infant organized these relations into self and object representations and then projected and reintrojected various aspects of these images. Understanding these processes clarifies the patient's relationships in the present because all such relationships are perceived and reacted to through the spectacles of these early organized self and object representations. The assumption here is that the infantile ego is capable of such organization; recent research on infants (Stern 1985) suggests that this is quite unlikely. Empirical investigation of infants carries the hope that, as we come to understand the capacities and limitations of the mind of the infant and child, we will have better criteria on which to choose or reject psychoanalytic models (Lichtenberg 1983).

3. A third channel, which focuses on the patient's being-in-the-world, I have labeled the *phenomenological* point of view. Here an attempt is made to grasp the facts of the patient's life "phenomenologically," that is, without other

theoretical preconceptions to organize the data. This approach was elaborated in philosophy by Husserl and then differently by Heidegger, and taken up especially by the pioneer psychoanalysts Boss (1963) and Binswanger (1963), especially in their effort to understand seriously disturbed and psychotic patients.

The confusing notion of phenomenology has been used in many ways. It was originally developed by Husserl under the influence of Brentano. According to Jones (1953), Freud attended Brentano's seminar in philosophy once a week for a couple of years. Husserl (1913) first used the term in 1900, and for him it was a way of doing philosophy, the phenomenologic method. A *phenomenon* is whatever appears for us immediately in experience. Husserl's method rests on what he calls *transcendental-phenomenological reduction*; he does not permit the selection out of experience of certain specific things, sensations, feelings, and so on, since to do so would assume classificatory principles about the world. Thus, phenomenological statements cannot be called empirical, because empirical statements are about already assumed "things" out there. Phenomenological statements attempt what Husserl calls *presuppositionless inquiry*—no theories, just descriptions of phenomena as they present themselves to an unprejudiced view.

Husserl (1913) defines phenomenological reduction as the "bracketing of existence," or *epoché*, the unbiased contemplation of phenomena without intellectual considerations. One must suspend belief in everything, use "imaginative variations," and then intuit the essence of the phenomena. Thus, phenomenological statements are not empirical; for Husserl they are statements about the intuitive essence of the phenomena.

From the point of view of the psychotherapist, the phenomenological stance is just to react to what is simply there in a felt experience; the therapist does not disconnect, isolate, or interpret aspects of this experience. *Epoché*, phenomenological reduction, or the bracketing of being, demands refrainment from judgment about morals, values, causes, background, and even the subject (the patient) and objective observer (the therapist). One pays special attention to one's own state of consciousness in the presence of a patient—for example, to the "feel" of a schizophrenic, the ambience such an individual creates.

Phenomenologist psychotherapists, such as R. D. Laing, attempt to bridge the gap between the couch and the analyst's chair by focusing on the effect of the therapist as a detached technician, who reinforces the patient's problems by becoming one more in a chain of powerful individuals who have pretended to take an interest in the patient. What is more and what is worse, they argue, is the demand that the patient too must pretend that this interest is real, while in truth both therapists and patients know that therapists' responses are all too often determined by their definition of themselves as therapists rather than by the feelings that the patient as a person arouses in them. Faced with this clinical detachment, the patient can only respond to what Laing (1960) cleverly calls the absence of the therapist's presence or, still more destructively, "the presence of the therapist's absence."

The point of this stance is that the therapist must continue to observe and listen in what they call the phenomenological sense, staying with the patient's material and taking everything the patient has to say at face value rather than searching for hidden processes; this is derived from the practice of *phenomenological reduction*. The phenomenologists' argument is that a distance is created between the therapist and the patient by the analytic technique of free association, and that this gap may be unproductively filled by abundant verbal material and abundant analytic ideas, conceptions, and theories. Instead they advise focusing on the emotional interchange based on staying strictly with the phenomena and the manifest appearance presented by the patient. Phenomenological reduction of the emotional distance between the patient and the therapist then, is the crucial procedure, leading to a true meeting or encounter (Jaspers 1972), hard to define but something we have all experienced.

The application of phenomenology to psychotherapy raises the valid question of whether we as therapists can be sure that we are seeing and hearing our patients as they really are, rather than as projections of our theories about them. The aim of phenomenological study is to rediscover the living person and the existential reality for that person.

Existential psychotherapy is another alternative paradigm, derived from, but not the same as, phenomenology. Because it downplays or discards Freud's unconscious, it is not psychoanalytic and I am not recommending it here. What we borrow in this book from phenomenology is a stance in which the notion of *dasein* is introduced, very loosely meaning human existence, human "being-there," from which comes the term *daseinanalyse*, the study of the patient's three modes of being in the world: (1) *umwelt*, our environment; (2) *mitwelt*, our fellow humans; and (3) *eigenwelt*, the mode of our relationship to ourselves. Every patient needs to be understood from all these modes of existence in the world. The term *dasein* is used instead of Descartes's *ego* or *cogito* to stress that we are always as human beings "there-beings," situated in the world, and not ever disinterested spectators of it.

Phenomenology is defined differently by each author, but central to the concept is the notion of our sensitivity to the unfolding of lived experience, an unfolding that we allow to show itself in its own manner without forcing our preconceptions onto it. What this led to in continental philosophy was a decentering of the individual human subject in various incompatible approaches such as those of Hegel, Feuerbach, Marx, and Nietzsche.

A psychological corollary of this third channel was elaborated by thinkers such as Fromm, Sartre, Foucault, and Lacan (reviewed by Chessick 1985a, 1987a,b): Society shapes the individual, and we can only understand individuals if we understand the society, culture, or world in which they must continuously live and interact. Thus, to understand an individual, we must understand that unique, lived state of being-in-the-world in all three aspects just mentioned. We must understand the cultural milieu, the ideology shared by the group, and the relationship of individuals implicit in the prevailing economic system. These aspects express themselves directly in the patient's thought and speech or, as Sartre in his later writing pointed out, are mediated through the family as it forms the child's personality. The notion of the unconscious is retained by some in this group of thinkers, especially Lacan, but it is viewed as being formed, not by drives, but as a consequence of having to fit into the social order. In order to do this, the truth of the person's desires becomes repressed and manifests itself in an ever more disguised form. The hidden assumptions, values, and background practices of the social order constitute the conscious, knowing subject and generate a false sense of freedom and "objective" perception of "facts." The Cartesian dichotomy between the knower or thinking subject *(cogito)* and the "objective world," upon which classical natural science is based, breaks down, and the human individual is "decentered."

4. The fourth approach is from *self psychology* (Kohut 1971, 1977, 1984), which focuses on the state of the patient's

self as it is empathically grasped by the analyst. Important originators of this approach were Fairbairn and Winnicott, who introduced the notion of the true and the false self, which was taken up in detail by Laing (1960) in his brilliant exposition of schizoid and schizophrenic conditions. Although numerous versions of the concept of self were already being used in philosophy and psychology, it was Kohut who brought the focus on the self into a systematic and elaborate psychoanalytic theory; significant alterations in this theory have recently been offered by Gedo (1979, 1984), whose work does not receive the attention it deserves. Although Gedo rejects many of Kohut's premises, often on the basis of excellent arguments, his establishment of hierarchies of self-organization represents a further elaboration upon and movement away from traditional psychoanalytic metapsychology, and his discussions contain arguments and proposals with which every therapist ought to be familiar.

Muslin and Val (1987) offer a straightforward introduction to Kohut's self-psychology approach for the practicing psychotherapist. They distinguish between cognitive observations and empathic observations, following a philosophical tradition that goes back to Dilthey, or perhaps to Vico. Cognitive observations are of verbal and nonverbal behaviors as well as of the therapist's subjective reactions, and are capable of being consensually validated by other objective observers. Empathy, on the other hand, is defined by Muslin and Val as "a mode of observation that attempts to capture the subject's inner life" (p. 5) and requires the observer to draw out of himself or herself a state of experience that somewhat approximates that of the subject. These assessments, claim the authors, allow the therapist to answer such questions as "What is the patient experiencing?" and "Where are these reactions coming from?"

The complexity and controversial aspects of the empathic approach to data gathering have been much discussed in philosophy and in psychotherapy literature, and Reed (1987) argues that the systems of self psychology and traditional psychoanalysis are not basically compatible. She also warns that "the classical analyst who listens only to resistance and the self psychologist who listens only to material relating to the empathic failure of a self-object are listening to theory, not the patient" (p. 437). She claims that self psychology derives meaning directly from the manifest content of the patient's material, whereas classical psychoanalysis requires in addition "that we rely on both the patient's free associations, and nonverbal communications such as reenactments" (p. 438). Thus classical theory moves toward uncovering "specific fantasy-memory constellations" (p. 442).

All these authors agree that the essential task is listening. For Muslin and Val, "the therapist must train himself to listen to the moment-to-moment connections and the associated nonverbal material of affect and action connected with the word associations" (p. 8). Listening requires the therapist to be free from the urges to "do" or to "say" something, an idea that runs contrary to much of medical training and to our prevailing pragmatic culture. It leaves the problem of validation of empathic observations to the internal process of the treatment, a form of hermeneutics rather than utilizing empirical scientific observation.

5. The fifth and final approach on which to base organization of the patient's communications might be loosely termed the *interactive* approach, which focuses on the therapist's countertransference, or, more generally, on the here-and-now factors in the treatment, emphasizing the analyst's participation. Schwaber's views, discussed in the first chapter,

represent an extreme example of this, although they are infused with Kohut's insistence on the primary role of the analyst's empathic grasp of how the patient experiences the analyst as constituting the methodology that distinguishes psychoanalysis from the other sciences; I would therefore place her approach in the fourth channel.

Many of the numerous and conflicting points of view placed under this "interactive" rubric have been developed as a response to our increasing understanding, especially in preoedipally damaged patients, of the patient's need for an experience and not just an explanation in the treatment. Modell (1976) offers the notion of the psychoanalytic process in the early phase of the treatment of narcissistic or schizoid patients as providing a "cocoon," a holding of the patient until the patient is ready for self-exploration. Langs (1982) emphasizes the presence of delineated interactive fields in which the patient's data is loaded with allusions to the therapist's participation and even to the therapist's mental state. In this extreme but carefully constructed view, the patient's unconscious is seen as having the capacity for perception of the therapist's personal difficulties and as motivated to cure the therapist so that the therapist may in turn cure the patient.

Gill (1982) in a less radical approach emphasizes the importance of the therapist's participation in determining the particular transference manifestations that develop in a given treatment, and he also focuses his interpretations very much on the here-and-now interaction between patient and therapist. Gill's view is close to Sullivan's (1947, 1953) more extreme interpersonal theory of psychiatry, which, however, erroneously eschews Freud's crucial concept of psychic reality and attempts to study a scientifically delineated interaction in the treatment, one in which the therapist simultaneously participates in and observes the interaction. Sullivan's approach suffers from a metapsychological shallowness because of its emphasis on the interactional without sufficient study of the filtering mechanism through which the patient inevitably experiences this interaction. Sullivan's (1947, 1953) concept of parataxic distortion attempts to make up for this, but it has not received widespread acceptance.

Nietzsche, a philosopher postulating a metaphysical notion of the principle of "will to power" underlying all human behavior and mentation, profoundly influenced Adler's psychoanalytic approach (Chessick 1977b, 1983b). Breaking with Freud, Adler attempted to evaluate psychoanalytic data on the basis of what he misunderstood as Nietzsche's interactive principle; his approach suffers from an intrinsic oversimplification of all explanations. I do not employ the concepts of Adler or Sullivan, or of the mystical Jung, in my work, since they represent the direct reading of manifest content, using clinically unverifiable or *a priori* generalizations.

Wolf (1985), from a self-psychological point of view, pointed out, in his notion of "regressive listening," the impact of the therapy situation itself on the analyst and his capacity to listen. This important concept belongs at the margin of the self-psychological and the interactive channels, and I hope it will receive greater attention and explication in the future. Wolf stresses the regression of both the patient and the analyst in psychoanalysis, the so-called regression in the service of the ego, and attends to their defenses against such regression. Writing from the point of view of self psychology, Wolf blames these defences on the fear of the dissolution of the self inherent in regression. Regression, as a precondition of reaching a state of evenly suspended attention and constraint of self-expression on the analyst's part, leads to a need to idealize the patient. This countertransference has a beneficial effect, since it confirms the patient's unrealized potential and motivates the patient to live up to it.

Blum (1983), on the other hand, warns that focus on transference and countertransference can be overdone, leading to a situation in which psychotherapy becomes an empty ritual, a narcissistic system reflecting the analyst's grandiosity. He urges carefully listening to delineate the "point of urgency," which may be the here-and-now of the patient's actual life situation, the sphere of the patient's external reality in all its aspects. He adds that there are also crucial reality factors operating in the transference itself, such as the countertransference or even the analyst's actual ego-syntonic character traits.

It is clear that the interactive channel is the most controversial and most poorly delineated in the literature. All theorists from the other four channels have something to say about it, but they all disagree on its characterization and importance, and they all describe it from their differing theoretical stances in an incompatible fashion. Let us turn in more detail to a clinical explication of this channel, without attempting to resolve these theoretical disagreements.

AN EXPERIENCE, NOT JUST AN EXPLANATION

Loewald (1986) was a pioneer in developing the traditional psychoanalytic approach, but he also insisted that the patient's experience of the analyst is a major factor in the curative process. How does this experience affect the process of psychoanalytic listening? For example, sometimes the patient's experience in the analytic situation is only revealed in what Gabbard (1982) has called the "exit line" of both the patient and the analyst. As the patient leaves the room at the end of a session, they engage in a "separate" type of dialogue or interaction, in which the patient directly exposes material that has been left out of awareness during the period of free association. This is also an especially valuable time to study countertransference manifestations (Chessick 1986b). Freud, as mentioned in Chapter 1, was aware of this phenomenon, at least as a clue to the transference.

Gedo (1977) sharpened our focus on the archaic transferences, in which the patient forces the analyst to respond, thus contaminating Freud's stance of evenly hovering attention. The management of such archaic transferences and their effect on psychoanalytic listening is one of the most important issues in modern psychoanalytic therapy, because so many patients present with preoedipal damage and rapidly develop such transferences. Gunther (1976) emphasizes the converse of the archaic transference—namely, the narcissistic aspects of the countertransference. Gunther points out that countertransference manifestations often appear after the therapist's narcissistic equilibrium has been upset; they represent an attempt to restore the therapist's equilibrium, and he urges us to look for these situations in psychoanalytic listening.

An insufficiently noted paper by Greenson (1974) emphasizes the nonverbal message communicated to the patient by analysts who work on a mass-production forty-five minute schedule. He reminds us of how the patient feels when he or she lies down on a couch that is still warm from the last patient, and he advocates the 50-minute hour in order to neutralize the message inherent in this mass-production method of treatment. This paper is often quoted, but its recommendations are rarely followed.

The most complete traditional exposition of the interaction between patient and analyst has been offered in a series of papers by Lipton (1977a, 1979, 1983), who goes back to a restudy of Freud's cases in order to demonstrate the ways in which significant aspects of the real interaction between the patient and the analyst profoundly affected the data that were presented for psychoanalytic listening. Thus Freud, in his actual practice, violated some of his own admonitions contained in his papers on technique. Stone (1961) systematized this under the rubric of the "physicianly vocation" of the analyst and has compellingly demonstrated the profound impact of this stance on the material produced and on the process of the treatment itself.

With this list of important contributions to a focus on patient–therapist interaction, reaching its extreme in the differing views of Langs and Schwaber, we see that Freud's early advocacy of neutrality and opacity to the patient represents a theoretical impossibility, and it can easily be demonstrated that even in his own work he did not follow these precepts. It is likely that Freud's papers on technique were aimed at preventing massive acting out by incompletely analyzed or even unanalyzed therapists with their patients, as was common in the early days of psychoanalysis and remains all too common, though with much less justification, today. Freud's admonitions, in the middle of the twentieth century in the United States, tended to become codified into a rigid set of rules that sometimes produced iatrogenic narcissistic manifestations in patients and led either to an impasse in the treatment or to a surrender of autonomy by the patient, accompanied by a massive identification with the "aggressor" analyst; obviously these are unsatisfactory outcomes for a lengthy and expensive treatment.

Many authors from various standpoints, including those mentioned in this chapter, have addressed this danger in their own way, but the conflicting premises behind their approaches again highlights the difference between viewing the patient as suffering from a psychic deficit, with emphasis on experiential repair, and viewing the patient as suffering from psychic conflict that requires explication. No effort will be made in this book to reconcile the differing premises on which these various modes of attunement are based, as indeed it is my conviction that they cannot at present be reconciled. What I will do in the chapters that follow is demonstrate the application of these various modes of attunement to achieve a broader understanding of clinical data and illustrate the ways in which the use of these five channels can lead to more effective understanding, with the salutary result of more appropriate interventions.

LIMITATIONS OF MY APPROACH

My view differs significantly from that of Gedo and Goldberg (1973) in that their principle of "theoretical complementarity" (p. 4) assumes that the differing frames of reference or models of the mind may operate only as long as no internal contradictions arise among the various parts of the theory. They believe that even Freud did not intend to dispense with his older conceptions as he went foward to propose new ones, and that the changeover from one set of Freud's concepts to another did not necessarily indicate that one replaced or superseded the other. These authors maintain that Freud

> correctly assumed that a given set of data might be understood most clearly by utilizing one particular frame of reference or

> model of the mind, whereas another set of data demanded a different set of concepts for its clarification. [p. 4]

In my approach, on the other hand, theoretical orientations are being used that *directly conflict with one another* and cannot be thought of as complementary because their basic premises, both their epistemological foundations (Chessick 1980b) and their basic assumptions about human nature and its motivations (Chessick 1977b), directly collide. This forces a radical discontinuity as we shift from channel to channel in our receiving instrument, rather than allowing us, as we would all prefer, to slide back and forth between theoretically consistent positions—or at least complementary positions that are consistent with one another.

The worst mistake a beginner in psychoanalytic listening can make at this historical point in the development of psychoanalytic theory is to assume that, in some fashion, these five standpoints can be blended or melded into some supraordinate theory that can generate all of them. Careful examination of the premises of these standpoints reveals that one composite theory is impossible in our current state of knowledge. We are forced, if we use this shifting of systems, to accept the radical discontinuities—much in the way the early physicists had to accept the fact that certain data involving light rays were better explained by wave theory, whereas other data were best explained by corpuscular theory—despite the fact that these two theories were radically incompatible in the prevailing state of scientific understanding at the time. The problem in the human sciences is even more profound, and some thinkers, such as Foucault (1973), have claimed that *in principle* agreement can never be reached on a single theoretical model for scientific understanding of all human mentation and behavior.

It may seem to some readers that certain other theoretical models should be added to these channels; what I am offering here is what has proven in my thirty years of clinical experience to be most valuable, to be the least speculative (or experience-distant), and to result in the least number of arbitrary inferences. The most important requirement of a model is that it be suggested by the very data the patient produces, rather than be superimposed on the data by the therapist's experience-distant, or arbitrary, or mystical, or dogmatic preconceptions. This is a relative concept because no theory is truly experience-near, since it is impossible to approach data without some preconceptions. Our only hope is that our preconceptions are not too abstract, generalized, and divorced from the specific material, and that they are capable of being validated by a study of the patient's responses to interventions based on them. Even this is fraught with difficulty, as it is all too human to hear what we wish to hear. Hence the value of consultation and of the publication of the details of therapist–patient exchanges in case reports, which all too often lack such information.

The most difficult task in using this approach is to be willing to keep discontinuous and conflicting models in one's mind; to do so offends the natural and very dangerous human tendency to insist upon a neat, consistent, holistic theoretical explanation of all material, even if it is wrong. Kant (1781) called this mental tendency the regulative principle of reason, Bacon (1620) called it "idols of the tribe," and Freud would have based it on the powerful synthesizing function of the ego. Tolerance and flexibility, as well as a certain maturity, are required on the part of the listener, and this can be very difficult to achieve, for it is sometimes the unfortunate result of an improperly conducted training or personal psychoanalysis that one becomes a rigid adherent of the particular theoretical orientation of one's analyst.

Kohut (1984) has suggested that the reasons for this

highly charged narcissistic investment in one point of view are inherent in a psychoanalysis that has incorrectly and prematurely interpreted certain transference manifestations. Unanalyzed selfobject transferences remain attached to post-analytic theories and schools of thought that attract the therapist. Since there are no data available at present that convincingly and decisively prove any of these theoretical orientations to be the one correct orientation, this uncritical and often irritable adherence would have to be a leftover of a misunderstood or unanalyzed transference, just as emerging from one's psychoanalysis with a sense of nihilism about all analytic theories would be a similar indication for further analytic work.

ATTEMPTS AT SYNTHESIS

Horney (1987), in her final lectures, emphasizes that the quality of the analyst's attention is the basis for good work. She delineates three aspects of the quality of attentiveness to the patient: wholeheartedness, comprehensiveness, and productiveness. Wholehearted attention is "difficult to attain," says Horney (p. 18). It involves not being distracted, being absorbed in one's work, "a being altogether with all one's faculties in the situation—and all concentrated on the work" (p. 118). Comprehensiveness of observation requires that the analyst avoid prematurely selecting what is significant or what should be interpreted. This is a special danger for those who approach the material with a rigid theoretical orientation, determined to find what they are convinced must be always there, looking for quick and easy connections.

Every possible observation must be registered before making selections, and Horney notes that such a demand may frighten the beginner. She reminds us that this situation is similar to that of learning to drive a car: At first there seem to be an overwhelming number of details that demand attention; yet the process eventually becomes automatic as the various tasks are mastered. An additional factor in analytic work is that as our understanding of the patient increases, our observations and impressions "fall into line, and the easier it becomes to pay attention to them" (p. 27).

This falling into line is also a function of the third aspect of the quality of attentiveness: productiveness. This strange quality taxes the resources of the analyst and involves the intensity of the meaning of the patient's material—an intensity that may suddenly appear in the midst of a "boring" session if one's resources are tapped. This is when the material falls into line. Such a process is interfered with by taking notes, remarks Horney, in agreement with Freud's comments on note taking quoted in Chapter 1.

Pine (1985) attempted to coordinate some of these channels of listening by relying on developmental theory. For Pine, diverse developmental moments lead to phenomena that are best addressed by one or the other of the listening stances that we have discussed. Each of the various theories addresses some aspect of developmental problems, and analysts must have in mind an array of concepts as they listen; the therapist is characterized as a "prepared explorer" (p. 204). Pine explains that he is not arguing for a random eclecticism in theories or for any particular theory. His point is that because of the diverse phenomena of each person's life and development, it follows, not that each listening channel will be equally relevant for every patient, but that "the analyst will gain from having in mind a diverse array of concepts that will permit him to hear the patient's material in variously organized ways" (pp. 68–69).

Although he probably would not agree with either Pine's

or my multiple approach, DeWald (1987) uses a similar attitude in supervision: "If the behavior persists, you sort of stand back and say to yourself, 'What meaning am I missing? What *else* does this thing mean?' " (p. 181). Coming up with new configurations and meanings, interpreting them to the patient, and observing the results of the interpretation constitute the core of the therapy process as DeWald conceptualizes it, forcing the therapist to constantly stand back and look for new meanings. The use of the five-channel approach proposed here I believe facilitates this indispensable process.

Thomä and Kächele (1985) attempted to provide a formal model of this process, conceptualizing psychoanalytic therapy as "an ongoing, temporally unlimited focal therapy with a changing focus" (p. 347). The focus is central to their "Ulm process model." They believe it to be interactionally formed and ever changing, regardless of whether it is reached by the analyst intuitively or from theoretical considerations. In this model they are describing the ever-changing focal topic of the analytic hours, but the analyst's personality and listening channel always have a profound influence: "We believe the sequence of the focusses to be the result of an unconscious exchange between the patient's needs and the possibilities open to the analyst" (p. 348).

All of this is consistent with the most powerful thinking in continental philosophy and psychology today. Gadamer's (1982) *Truth and Method*, a central work in hermeneutic theory, was significantly based on Heidegger's (1962) account of understanding in *Being and Time*. Gadamer points out that understanding is essentially anticipative; it envisages and preconceives the meaning of what is to be interpreted. This is a modern statement of the paradox of Plato's dialogue *Meno*; in current terminology, we might say that anyone who "understands" communications exists first in a historically determinate relationship to that which is to be understood and is historically bound to tradition and language at the time. The attempt to avoid this situation in the natural sciences presupposes a certain alienation or distancing from the subject under investigation, with a loss of the more primordial relation of participation. Thus, in our attempts to be objective or scientific, there is always a tension between alienating distanciation and the experience of participation. As Heidegger puts it, our understanding of communication is permanently determined by the anticipatory movement of fore-understanding. This paradox, though inescapable (Chessick 1986a), can be reduced by consciously accepting what Gadamer (1982) called, nonpejoratively, "prejudices" (p. 238), and by attempting to view the material from a series of irreconcilable stances, rather than holding fast to one set of prejudgmental anticipations. As Gadamer explains, "The important thing is to be aware of one's own bias, so that the text may present itself in all its newness and thus be able to assert its own truth against one's own fore-meanings" (p. 238).

THREE

LISTENING TO THE PSYCHOTIC PATIENT

THIS CHAPTER PRESENTS several case studies to illustrate the most difficult task of all: learning to listen to the psychotic patient. We will begin with the case of Ellen West, published by the famous existential psychiatrist Binswanger (1958). This is one of the most fascinating and useful cases in all of psychiatric literature, as it presents an immense volume of carefully collected information, followed by a substantial phenomenological and existential discussion of the data. It also documents some of the most blatant mishandling of a patient that can be found in published case reports; for that alone it is worth careful examination, since it teaches us that the psychotic patient has an uncanny capacity—perhaps through projective identification—to generate destructive countertransference problems.

Kernberg (1987) provides excellent case demonstrations of the enormous countertransference feelings and states evoked by such patients. Using the object relations approach, he dramatically emphasizes the importance of the therapist's continuing awareness of the specific feelings being engendered in the therapist by the patient. A lack of this awareness leads to the danger of countertransference acting out, in which the therapist may actually behave consistently with the role that is projected onto him or her—with consequences that are always deleterious and sometimes, as we will see in the case of Ellen West, calamitous.

THE CASE OF ELLEN WEST

Ellen West is described as the only daughter of a 66-year-old Jewish father "for whom her love and veneration know no bounds" (p. 237). She had a younger brother and a brother four years older than she; at the age of 17, the younger brother suffered a mental ailment characterized by suicidal ideation, but he recovered. Ellen described her father as very self-controlled, formal, and reserved. Outwardly he was a willful man of action, but internally he was soft and suffered from depression, fear, and self-reproach. There was a history of depression, suicide, and other mental illness in the father's family. Ellen's mother was described as "a very soft, kindly, suggestible nervous woman, who underwent a depression for three years during the time of her engagement" (p. 238). The impression is that both mother and father were depressed, nervous, and fearful during Ellen's childhood. Little information was available about the first ten years of Ellen's life; we are told, however, that at 9 months she refused milk, and that she was a headstrong, defiant, and even violent child.

Ellen was quite interested in poetry and wrote many letters and poems to her friends, parents, and therapists. One of the most striking aspects of her history is that although she took a number of trips, she could never be comfortable away from her parents. When she was 20 years old, her father forced her to break an engagement to a foreigner; afterward she was tormented by the idea that she was getting too fat, and she was continuously depressed. She kept a lengthy diary. Her symptoms had become progressively worse by the time she was 23, and she developed a profound dread of getting fat, which painfully conflicted with an intensified longing for food, especially sweets. This conflict began to preoccupy her continuously.

She entered into an affair with a student and became engaged to him. Her parents opposed the engagement, and she became severely depressed. She took 36 to 48 thyroid tablets daily in an effort to remain thin. When she was 25 years old, the engagement was broken. At 26 she developed a love for music and entertained plans to marry a cousin, while at the same time dating the student to whom she had been engaged. She remained depressed and hated her body, often beating it with her fists. At the age of 28, she finally broke off entirely with the student and married her cousin.

For the next four years her life was preoccupied with a conflict over pregnancy, which she wanted but which was thought to be prevented because of her inability to get herself to eat properly. She developed an intense interest in social welfare, an increasingly profound depression, and a preoccupation with diet and laxatives. A turning point occurred at the age of 31 when, "during a hike with her husband, suddenly, with elemental force, the confession bursts from her that she is living her life only with a view to being able to remain thin, that she is subordinating every one of her actions to this end, and that this idea has gained a terrible power over her" (pp. 248–249).

The Story Of Her Treatment

At the age of 32, Ellen began her first psychoanalysis "with a young and sensitive analyst who is not completely committed to Freud" (p. 249). She seemed to become less depressed under the influence of this analysis, but it was noted that when her husband was absent, her former nursemaid had to stay with her. Although she claimed that the psychoanalysis was useless, she shared the analyst's opinion that her main goal was to subjugate others. During the analysis she became obsessed with food and tormented by feelings of dread. At the same time she seemed less preoccupied by the wish to die. When she was 33, the analysis was discontinued in its seventh month "for external reasons," and she developed a state of severe dread and agitation. It became necessary for her to undergo treatment with a second analyst, who is described as "more orthodox than the first" (p. 252).

> This description of the second analyst seems to be contradicted by the following paragraph in the history, in which we are told that the analyst requested her husband not to continuously stay with her even though he wished to stay. This hardly sounds orthodox. When the husband left her presence in obedience to the analyst, the patient attempted suicide. "The analyst ascribes no importance to this attempt and continues with the analysis" (p. 252). The patient made a second suicide attempt, and at one point, tried to

> throw herself out of a window in the analyst's office. This apparently resulted in her return to her husband and a move into an internist's clinic.*

It should be noted that in Europe at this time, the family of a wealthy patient, and sometimes even their servants, lived in the medical institution with the patient, so this move is not in itself extraordinary. At this point the patient was under the care of both an internist and the analyst; she lived with her husband in the internist's clinical establishment.

> Her "orthodox" analyst advised her to keep a diary. The essence of the material in the diary is that she attempts to satisfy two needs by eating: hunger and love. "Hunger gets satisfied–love does not! There remains the great, unfilled hole" (p. 254).

It is clear that the patient is not undergoing an orthodox psychoanalysis, but the relevant issue for us is how one ought to listen to the material she presents. From the classical psychoanalytic point of view, the patient was suffering from a profound preoedipal disorder, although at the time it was thought of as a severe obsessional neurosis, the justification for the psychoanalysis. It would be difficult to maintain that this represents a regression from a primarily oedipal problem rather than a structural deficit, although we were told at the start of the history about the patient's boundless love and veneration for her father. Some authors (Wilson 1983) believe that these severe cases of anorexia, with their obsessive concerns over food and their phobic dread of being fat, represent a regression from a primarily oedipal disorder. In this case, if

---

*Please note that throughout this book, detailed case material appears in a different type to set it off from my annotations.

we were to follow such a traditional approach, the patient's incestuous feelings toward her father would eventually have to be interpreted. We are given very little information about the transference; the analyst's focus seems to be on gathering endless data in the form of journal entries, poems, and an extended anamnesis from this patient.

> Because the psychoanalyst believed the case to be one of an obsessional neurosis, he made some interpretations about anal erotism, which the patient found "completely incomprehensible" (p. 254).

From an object relations point of view, one might stress the patient's need to cling to her husband (and in his absence her nursemaid or her parents). It represents at this point a classic example of a borderline problem involving separation and individuation, and an attempt on the part of the patient to reenact separation and return in the drama of control over the food that goes into and out of her body. The focus in this approach would be on preoedipal incorporation fantasies and the patient's hidden aggression, which could help to account for her inability to allow her husband or mother or nursemaid out of her sight for a moment. Certainly this aggression was destroying the patient's life, and the case is open to Kleinian types of interpretation, beginning with the fact that her conflict between wanting pregnancy and wishing to remain thin after she got married seems to have precipitated the downhill course of events. Consciously the patient wished to be pregnant, but she was unable to countenance the responsibilities of caring for an infant because she had so many unmet needs of her own, and she was preoccupied with dealing with them through her dramatic eating disorder. The wish to become pregnant and the interest in social work represented a healthier effort to deal with her emptiness, but they were overshadowed by the obsession with eating, vomiting, laxatives, thyroid pills, and so on. Regardless of which channel of listening—Freudian or Kleinian—was employed, the approach to the case would still be traditionally psychoanalytic, and only the focus of the interpretations would be different.

From the point of view of self psychology, the emphasis would be on the soothing caretaker. The parents, the student, the husband, the nursemaid, and, for a short period, both the interest in music and the first analyst—all had a soothing effect on her agitation and dread. The self psychologist might focus on the patient's inability to deal with her inner tensions by herself and her need for an external source of calm and strength with which she could merge in an idealizing transference. The issue of idealization actually did come up in the case (p. 250): The patient at times idealized her husband and at other times idealized her rejected student-lover, and she was acutely aware of the times when these idealizations were disappointed. The patient had also received a good deal of direction from various authoritative individuals, including her father, her second analyst, and her internist. She appeared to slip easily into a condition of ambivalence, dependency, and obedience to such authority figures, but she somehow left all of them feeling helpless and impotent.

> The patient became increasingly disappointed with her analysis. She reported that at the age of 32, she had already received her first "inkling of the fact that I had become enslaved to an uncanny power which threatened to destroy my life" (p. 257) and that by age 33, her psychoanalysis, which was undertaken in an attempt to free herself of this power, was not successful: "Analysis was a disappoint-

> ment. I analyzed with my mind, and everything remained theory. The wish to be thin remained unchanged in the center of my thinking" (p. 257). The patient's life became a hell in which she was obsessed with the issue of eating. Kraeplin was consulted and he diagnosed melancholia. "The analyst considers this diagnosis incorrect and continues the analysis" (p. 257).

There were now three medical authorities working on the case of this patient: the second analyst, the internist, and Kraeplin. Each had a different opinion. Meanwhile the analyst continued his treatment. There is no detailed discussion of the effect on the patient's communicated analytic material of having three medical authority figures, all of whom were concerned with her, and all of whom differed with one another.

> Ellen was "torn to and fro" by the differing views of the doctors regarding her illness and her treatment. The internist, "who judges the illness most correctly," insisted that she remain in the hospital, while the analyst advised "leaving the clinic and 'returning to life.' This advice completely shakes her faith in the analyst" (p. 257).

Clearly this analyst, whether labeled orthodox or not, appears to have acted out a countertransference in which he takes steps to manage his patient's life, rather than proceeding in the traditional analytic manner of allowing the patient to make her own decisions. The loss of confidence in the analyst is engendered by his poor listening to the patient's material; his advice to leave the hospital clearly represents a misunderstanding of the depth of the patient's pathology and the serious danger in which she finds herself.

> The internist intervened decisively, prohibited the continuation of the analysis, to which the patient agreed, and had her transferred to the Bellevue Sanitarium in Kreuzlingen, where she was apparently first seen by Binswanger. Here it was noted that her condition improved "during the constant presence of her husband, who has a very favorable effect on her" (p. 259). The second analyst sent a detailed report in which he diagnosed the patient as a case of severe obsessive neurosis with manic-depressive oscillations. He stated that he was convinced that the patient was "on the way to a cure!" (p. 260). He reported that anal erotism was the focus of her treatment, and he claimed that she recognized the relationship between chocolate and anal erotism as well as the equation that eating is the same as being fertilized, which is the same as being pregnant, which is the same as being fat. The analyst reported that the transference "then became so clear that on one occasion she sat down quite suddenly on the analyst's lap and gave him a kiss" (p. 260). On another occasion she wished him to call her "Ellen-child." We are also told that interpretations were attempted centering on her father complex and her incest wish, but "no material could be obtained, not even from her dreams. The infantile amnesia, unfortunately, was not illuminated by either analysis" (p. 260). He noted without comment that the analysis deteriorated as a sequel to their discussion of the patient's "father complex."

This is a dramatic example of poor psychoanalytic listening. The interpretations about the father complex are not based on any real clinical material, but come out of the analyst's theoretical preconception. We cannot blame Freud for advocating this poor technique because a study of Freud's cases (see Chapter 5) conclusively shows that his interpretations were almost always carefully focused on, or at least began with, the material at hand, and, later on, especially the transference. In the case of Ellen West, interpretive work would have first centered around the patient's continual reports of depressive inner torment and self-hatred, inability to be alone, and obsessive complaints, with the phrasing and emphasis depending on the channel of listening chosen by the analyst. Direct "id" interpretations would not be made, except perhaps by some Kleinians.

The patient's reported behavior toward the analyst constitutes a response to his parental acting out and cannot be construed as definitive evidence for an incestuous transference. This treatment can only be characterized as a wild analysis. It should be noted here that although this case was published in 1944, Kraeplin died in 1926, so the treatment was carried out by two analysts trained early in our century, at least 75 years ago. We know this since the patient was also attended by Kraeplin. Therefore no implications about psychoanalysis as it is practiced today can be drawn from this case.

> It turned out that Kraeplin's diagnosis was correct: The patient was suffering from a psychotic melancholia, of which the obsessive agitation was only one clinical feature. She stated, "Everything agitates me, and I experience every agitation as a sensation of hunger, even if I have just eaten" (p. 261). She reported the feeling that "all inner life has ceased, that everything is unreal, everything senseless . . . she wishes for nothing so much as to be allowed to go to sleep and not wake up again" (p. 261). Four dreams were recorded about five weeks later, but Binswanger states that "for psychotherapeutic reasons, an analysis of her dreams was not made" (p. 263).

The dreams are too long to quote in detail here, but they involved violence, eating, and suicide. No associations to the dream material were gathered "for psychotherapeutic reasons" (p. 321); what that means is not explained. What is clear is that even the patient now recognized that she suffered from melancholia, a severe agitated major depression.

> Her obsessions began to shift from food to death and suicide. An interesting observation intrudes itself on the reader at this point. In spite of this shift, Binswanger simply gathered more and more information from the husband and from the patient's journal entries: "In response to my request her husband gathers together the following material on the theme of suicide" (p. 265).

It seems clear that Binswanger is giving up hope on this patient and is simply gathering information rather than making active interpretive efforts. We are given no explanation as to his notion of what psychotherapy with this now-suicidal patient should comprise. From the traditional analytic point of view, the patient is telling us that she is increasingly angry and despairing, and that she is trying to defend against these feelings and to communicate them by the obsessional ideas, suicidal thoughts, and agitation.

From the object relations point of view, the suspicion inserts itself in the reader's mind that the patient, by projective identification, is inducing in Binswanger the same sense of frustration and hopelessness that she increasingly feels as these idealized medical authority figures, her husband, and earlier in life her parents seem to her more and more incapable and inept. We are told at this point that the wish to die runs through her entire life, and she seems to infect her caretakers with her despair and transform them into inadequate, passive mothers who cannot metabolize the data she presents to them. They cannot really listen to it, they cannot process it, and therefore they cannot return it to her in a form that she can use for ego expansion, growth, and development.

From a self-psychological point of view, interpretations would center on her increasing disappointment in idealized selfobjects and could even be linked with experiences of her early disappointments in her parents. She demands from all of them their continued soothing presence and a magical capacity to fill the empty hole, the empty, depleted self. Since no one can do this for her, the patient is bound to experience rage and empty depletion as an impending, unbearable dissolution of her self.

An interactive channel of listening becomes especially important at this time. The patient is evoking a sense of hopelessness and impotence in Binswanger. If, rather than interpreting, he were to act out these feelings by presenting a hopeless demeanor and an inept passivity (thus actualizing the projection), perhaps in order to avoid facing her rage and manipulativeness, the clinical consequences for the patient would surely be deleterious.

> Binswanger was a keen clinician. He realized that the patient was at increasing suicidal risk and requested permission from the patient's husband to transfer her to the closed ward; otherwise they would have to leave the institution. A very peculiar interchange then took place: "The very sensible husband saw this perfectly, but said he could give his permission only if a cure or at least a far-reaching improvement of his wife could be promised him" (p. 266). Binswanger responded that on the basis "of the anamnesis and my own observations I had to diagnose a progressive schizophrenic psychosis . . . I could offer the husband very little hope" (p. 266). He parenthetically adds that even if shock therapy had then existed, it would have offered only a

> temporary postponement of the dilemma, "but it would certainly have changed nothing in the final result" (p. 266). Binswanger was unshakably convinced that this patient would kill herself. He was also convinced that a release from the institution meant certain suicide. In order to share the responsibility, he called for another consultation, this time with Professor E. Bleuler "and a foreign psychiatrist." Bleuler agreed with the diagnosis of schizophrenia and both agreed completely with Binswanger's prognosis and "doubt any therapeutic usefulness of commitment even more emphatically than I . . . We therefore resolved to give in to the patient's demand for discharge" (p. 266). The patient was reported to be relieved by their willingness to discharge her; she went home and three days later took poison and died.

So ends one of the most extraordinary case reports ever published. According to Binswanger, these famous psychiatrists sent the patient to her death for the simple reason that they felt it was unavoidable! From an object relations stance, one might ask whether there was a countertransference acting out of a projective identification. More accurately, this patient, whose main goal was "to subjugate other people," produced a "projective counteridentification" (Grinberg 1979) in her male authority figures, all of whom were ordinarily active and vigorous. They acted this out by passively allowing the patient to commit suicide—an act of omission, so to speak, arising out of their being "stuck" in a temporary projective counteridentification. In this process, as Grinberg (1979) defines it, the therapist feels unavoidably transformed either into an object determined by the patient or into experiencing affects such as anger, depression, or anxiety "forced onto him" by the analysand (p. 174). According to Grinberg, this represents a specific response to "violent projective identification from the patient, which is not consciously perceived by the analyst" (p. 174). Furthermore, the analyst will use all sorts of rationalizations to justify the transformation.

THE DANGER OF A SINGLE-CHANNEL APPROACH

Therapists listening on any of the four channels beside the phenomenological one might have picked up an entirely different set of signals from this patient and certainly would not have so easily yielded to such therapeutic despair. Clearly Ellen should have been committed to the closed ward, and if the husband had refused permission, legal steps should have actively been undertaken to make some effort to force commitment in order to save the patient's life.

Where was the error? It was in the fact that these therapists listened to this patient using *only* the phenomenological channel, a channel that can be very useful in some situations but that tends to view behavior as a matter of conscious choice. For example, Binswanger (1958) writes:

> We must neither tolerate nor disapprove of the suicide of Ellen West, nor trivialize it with medical or psychoanalytic explanations, nor dramatize it with ethical or religious judgments. [p. 292]

This is one of those central philosophical issues that divides therapists. In my judgment, we should make every effort each time to prevent a patient from committing suicide because suicide is neither a simple matter of conscious choice nor a necessary or inherently unavoidable end to life. Binswanger's argument that Ellen's suicide was the result of the fact that her existence had become "ripe for death" (p. 295) is patent nonsense. Later (p. 298) he argues that only in her decision to die, did she find herself and choose herself. Indeed, the long, complicated "existential analysis" that serves as the second part of the case report can be thought of as a rationalization for the analysts' allowing the patient to go home and commit suicide, knowing full well that she would do so.

It is not difficult to see that an attitude of hopelessness, when communicated to the patient so blatantly, has in itself a devastating effect on the patient's self-esteem and represents almost an encouragement for the patient to commit suicide so as to somehow close the case. In the phenomenological literature, authenticity carries with it a connotation of something superior to inauthenticity. Although Heidegger (1962) used these Kierkegaardian terms in his "existential analytic" of human being, which so profoundly influenced continental philosophy, psychology, and psychoanalysis, he repeatedly insisted that this was not so. But when existentialist therapists talk about a patient's becoming authentic, they imply praise of the patient and an encouragement to go in that direction; in the case of Ellen West, Binswanger was convinced that she was most authentic when she committed suicide.

He writes: "The entire life-history of Ellen West is nothing but the history of the metamorphosis of life into mold and death" (p. 318). I believe that the entire history of Ellen West is a tragic demonstration of what can go wrong in the treatment of a psychotic patient when psychoanalytic listening is improperly carried out, and serves as a dramatic illustration of the dangers of listening on only one channel—no matter how expert the listener may be in the use of that single channel. There is nothing authentic or inevitable about a severely mentally ill patient's deciding to kill herself.

Understanding Ellen West's Eating Disorder

At the end of her life, Ellen West displayed a spectrum of borderline, affective, and schizophrenic features. Earlier in her history she would represent an extreme example of a severe mixed personality disorder including obsessional symptoms, anorexia, a binge-purge cycle, and phobias, all of which progressed to increasingly severe depression and paranoid delusions.

Self psychologists might say that the dramatic eating disorder, whether through alimentary orgasms (Chessick 1960), masochistic infliction of self-starvation or unpleasant compulsive stuffing, or the binge-purge guilt and restitution cycle, drains the rage and paranoia and focuses the patient's attention away from the empty, depleted self and onto preoccupation with gastrointestinal-tract sensations. In this manner, some sense of being alive is maintained. Thus on top of the depleted and fragmented nuclear core, the patient has built various protective rituals and soothing activities that, in the case of eating disorders, sometimes permit the patient to function in society.

At the same time, however, the patient must deal with massive narcissistic rage or unconscious sadism. The object relations channel would focus on this area of conflict. For example, Offenkrantz and Tobin (1974) discuss these patients as "depressive characters" and emphasize their great unconscious rage at important objects who are not providing them with what they unconsciously feel they need—and this rage is often turned on the therapist. Under this lies an "anaclitic depression" characterized by depletion and a hopelessness that gratification will never be sufficient.

Glover (1956) placed less emphasis on fixation in the oral stage and viewed addiction as a transition state between psychotic and neurotic phases, serving the function of controlling sadism and preventing a regressive psychosis, or fragmentation. He writes:

> The necessary formula appears to be that the individual's own hate impulses, together with identifications with objects towards whom he is ambivalent, constitute a dangerous psychic state . . . symbolized as an internal concrete substance. The drug is then . . . an external countersubstance which cures by destruction. In this sense drug-addiction might be considered an improvement on paranoia: the paranoidal element is limited to the drug-substance which is then used as a therapeutic agent to deal with intrapsychic conflict of a melancholic pattern. [p. 208]

In this form of "*localizing* paranoid anxiety," adaptation is enabled to proceed, and Glover postulates that the differences in choice of substance from the more benign, like food, to the dangerous, like chemicals, are simply related to the degree of archaic sadism. There is no compelling evidence for this postulate.

In my clinical experience (Chessick 1985a,b), the most serious problem in the intensive psychotherapy of eating disorders is not that of a schizophrenic loss of reality testing, as Bruch (1973) suggests, but of a deep characterological depression, often with core paranoid features, manifested primarily by a fixed derogatory self-image, cynicism, and hopelessness. All of this is reinforced by the long-standing nature of the condition, as well as by a profound narcissistic rage that begins to show itself as the eating disorder itself is corrected. Thus a long and difficult intensive psychotherapy is to be expected with such patients, because we are dealing with a profound preoedipal disorder characterized by severe, early structural defects. The case of Ellen West is an extreme example of such a disorder.

TWO SOURCES OF TRANSMISSION FOR PSYCHOANALYTIC LISTENING

Kernberg (1987) points out that analytic listening requires that we be tuned in to two sources of information. First there are direct communications of subjective experiences as patients speak freely about what is going on in their minds. Kernberg, borrowing from Racker (1968) and using the object relations stance, points out that under the usual conditions, in response to this material, "transitory concordant and complementary identifications" (p. 800) take place in the therapist's emotional reactions to the patient. These "realistic" reactions to the patient's transference enable therapists to empathize with the patient and expand their knowledge of the patient.

Concordant identifications reproduce experiences from the analyst's own past, facilitating empathy and leading to a sublimated positive concordant countertransference. Complementary identifications occur when the patient's internal objects evoke the analyst's neurotic remnants as if they were his or her own, and lead to complementary countertransference, in which the analyst reacts to these internal objects in the patient in a transferential fashion. Hunt and Issacharoff (1977) summarize Racker's concepts. They also mention a third form of countertransference, "indirect countertransference," which arises from the therapist's experiences with a third party (such as a spouse) who is central to the patient. These countertransferences are not reactions to projective identification. Self-analysis of such countertransferences can lead the analyst to greater knowledge of the patient's internal objects.

A second source of information arises from the patient's nonverbal behavior or from the patient's use of words as a means of action rather than for communication. Words here are used to directly express unconscious drives and defenses. Kernberg maintains that "the more severe the character pathology, the more nonverbal behavior predominates" (p. 801). These communications activate in the therapist "powerful affective dispositions reflecting what the patient is projecting" (p. 801).

The detection of projective identification, which is usually "employed in modeling" (p. 801) these nonverbal aspects of the patient's communication, depends on the analyst's alertness to the interpersonal implications of the patient's behavior and sensitivity to the activation of powerful and often very uncomfortable countertransference feelings; all this may be heard on the object relations channel as reflecting the patient's projections. Using this object relations stance therefore requires that analysts be willing to freely experience and investigate their own feelings and fantasies, no matter how unpleasant or unacceptable, as they are being evoked in the interaction with the patient.

As explained in Chapter 2, there is a blend here of interactive and object relations channels when one tunes in to projective identification, because the nonverbal interaction or the use of words in the nonverbal sense for action rather than communication constitutes an interpersonal experience that evokes in the analyst certain fantasies or feelings. Ego psychologists refer to this as the reinstinctualization of language, using the drive/conflict/defense orientation. As demonstrated in the case of Ellen West, in extremely disturbed patients these projected feelings can lead to dangerous misjudgments and to countertransference acting out that actualizes the projection. Such "externalization" (A. Freud 1965) is a frequent problem in the psychotherapy of borderline patients (Chessick 1972).

HOW KRAEPLIN MISSED A PARODY OF HIMSELF

The literature is replete with misunderstandings of patients caused primarily by therapists' inability to recognize what is evoked in themselves by the patient's communications. One of the most dramatic examples comes from Laing (1969), who borrows an account given by Kraeplin in 1905 to a lecture room full of his students. Kraeplin purports to demonstrate a patient who shows signs of catatonic excitement. Kraeplin emphasizes the patient's "inaccessibility." According to Kraeplin, although the patient undoubtedly understood all the questions he was asked, he gave no useful information; he provided "only a series of disconnected sentences having no relation whatever to the general situation" (p. 30).

By carefully reviewing the actual transcript of the patient's material, Laing (1960) makes it clear that the patient is carrying on a dialogue "between his own parodied version of Kraeplin, and his own defiant rebelling self" (p. 31). The patient obviously deeply resents the interrogation that Kraeplin is carrying out before a room full of students, and he is very much aware of being exhibited as a specimen:

> The patient sits with his eyes shut, and pays no attention to his surroundings. He does not look up even when he is spoken to, but he answers beginning in a low voice, and gradually screaming louder and louder. When asked where he is, he says, "You want to know that too? I tell you who is being measured and is measured and shall be measured. I know all that, and could tell you, but I do not want to." [p. 30]

This tenor continues throughout the interview, with the patient answering Kraeplin's question "What is your name?"

with a scream, "What is your name?" He begins to talk about shutting his eyes and being impudent and makes it clear, as he directs a stream of invectives against himself, that he is imitating what Kraeplin is thinking as he refuses to communicate. He is objecting to being measured and tested. Instead, as Laing says, "he wants to be heard" (p. 31).

A PSYCHOTIC PATIENT ATTEMPTS TO COMMUNICATE WITH KAHLBAUM

Another example of an inability to listen to psychotic patients can be found in the classic monograph *Catatonia* by Kahlbaum (1973). We are offered a case history of Paul M., who at the time of observation in 1866 was 24 years old. At the age of 20, he apparently had an acute psychotic episode characterized by hallucinations and delusions; he believed that he was "Misfortune" or "Typhoid," and he saw the Maid of Orleans standing in her petticoat on an inverted balloon. This terrifying acute psychosis lasted about seven months, after which he was discharged, apparently cured, and resumed his merchant business.

Two or three years later, the patient began to feel that his brain was being torn into a thousand pieces, and he had to discontinue his work as a merchant. A continuous struggle over masturbation had taken place in this man's life since the age of 14, forming an obsession very similar to Ellen West's struggle with food and eating. Kahlbaum describes the patient as displaying "a moral hangover and deep melancholy" (p. 35). He was readmitted to the hospital, but this time there was no significant improvement in his condition, although we are told he was discharged from the institution after approximately six months. He was unable to return to work.

Apparently because of a general apathy that annoyed his relatives, he was readmitted to the hospital for a third time. His physician asked him to write a summary of the relationship between masturbation and the history of his own life and illness. To the apparent surprise of the physicians, the content of the essay was quite logical, but evidently no attention was paid to it, nor was it used in any form of therapy. Here again, as in the case of Ellen West, there seems to be much emphasis on collecting historical information, almost for its own sake, perhaps in the hope that it would suddenly illuminate the case. Yet no serious study of the patient's material was carried out.

> Upon readmission, the patient began to attempt new communications. He refused to go out of the building into the open air. After five days he began to say strange things, such as, "I am in fact a man of fate" or "Things have been hidden from me which were quite interesting." The patient described his father as a hypochondriac and a closed personality, and his mother as taciturn. He insisted that he had been told as a child that he should become an actor. He added that he could be a sculptor, or a painter, or a singer, or an actor. He was sad but still hopeful and he concluded that "it may perhaps still be possible to overcome the consequences of the unfortunate impulses and to channel them in another direction" (p. 35). Apparently he had begun to talk about masturbation when Kahlbaum interrupted to state that he could rely completely on the listening physician's discretion. The patient replied, "Then I can make my confessions public."

In this famous monograph, written in 1874, masturbation is regarded as a moral issue, and the physicians are clearly very uncomfortable with the whole matter. A patient who masturbates continually from the age of 14 to the age of 25 is looked upon by the physicians as a kind of specimen and is considered to have a defect in will power; there is an interesting parallel to the presentation of Ellen West. Even a Freudian listening stance is interfered with at this point by the physicians' moral concerns and their assumption that the patient might not trust them to keep his grave secret, mostly a reflection of their own anxiety.

Listening from an object relations stance, we hear the patient evoking in the doctors a sense of his being disgusting and unpleasant, a kind of subhuman specimen to be kept at arm's length.

Self psychologists would emphasize the patient's intense effort to soothe himself through masturbation and his desperate effort to preserve some sense of self by slipping into an increasingly grandiose and exalted state. This apparent grandiosity escalated after his tearful description of his disappointing and ungiving parents. Yet his comments also ended with hope. If we listen on the interactive channel, what stands out is the doctor's interruption as the patient began to talk about masturbation. What reaction is to be expected from the patient at this point, and why? Before continuing, I urge the reader to close this book and try to imagine the patient's subsequent speech and behavior. . . .

> The patient suffered confusion and increasing physical agitation, which developed the following day into a catatonic excitement. During this time he ran around with much arbitrary striking out, shouting, and talking; he claimed that he wanted to see blood. However, Kahlbaum perceptively notes, "It was always clear that he did not have

> any real malicious intentions, because he never, for instance, struck anybody near him" (p. 36).

Clearly the patient was acting! In other words, just as he believed that the doctors were acting, both by professing an interest in listening to him, which they did not really have, and by telling him that he could rely completely on their discretion, while they were actually uncomfortable with, and were planning to publish his case with the story of his masturbation, he in turn presented them with an imitation and caricature of violence and anger. It was his way of simultaneously demonstrating that they were not listening to him, regressing to an archaic grandiosity of exhibiting himself as an actor and singer and sculptor and painter, hoping to evoke some kind of mirroring response, and at the same time demonstrating ego capacities to control and channel his anger and disappointment into a theatrical performance as an alternative to totally losing control.

The Loss of Hope and Its Consequences

> Even this dramatic behavior was met by the doctors with uncomprehending notes and observations but with no effort to actually communicate with the patient. They experienced him only as an offensive neuropathological specimen. Giving up all hope, he oscillated between periods of rage and periods of apathy or catatonic stupor.

The patient was feeling hopeless and shifted between dramatic exhibitions of himself, communications of his anger at not being listened to, and relapses into periods of hopeless despair. What impends is the calamity of fragmentation of the self.

> The patient stated, "When the principle has been disturbed, one's life is turned upside down" (p. 36). He also commented that he was a great man, a part of world history. The doctors noted his "revolting dirtiness (e.g., he consistently relieved himself next to the chamber-pot, and rubbed feces on his head)" (p. 36). At other times he spoke continuously and loudly to himself and assumed strange, fixed, awkward poses.

This is the typical deterioration of a patient who has lost hope. In the most primitive fashion, and yet with his characteristic sense of drama, using a method even more archaic than projective identification, he was still attempting to convey to the psychiatrists a sense of how terrible he felt about himself. At the same time, his being "revolting" evoked some kind of mirroring response in those around him. Again we are dealing with the last remnants of an effort to relate to other human beings. When all else fails, he speaks loudly to himself and begins to use primitive magic gestures and poses.

> This was abruptly followed by several days during which he was lucid and thoughtful. It soon terminated in the delusion that he was the natural child of his father and of his father's sister, and that this was a great secret. The patient stated that it was this fact that justified his mental disease.

This patient's effort to communicate to the psychiatrists is amazing. It is not possible to guess at the precise meaning of his central delusion, which eliminates his mother and makes him the child of his father's incest, but it is fascinating to see this obviously intelligent individual attempt to piece together and reconstitute his fragmented self and justify his mental illness in some fashion. Using the various listening channels to examine this last set of communications, we still can only speculate, because we do not have enough information; what is clear is that he is offering a number of leads to be followed, and earlier he even cooperated by writing down considerable material at the doctors' request.

Nothing was done with this material, however, and no real effort was made to make sense of his communications. This illustrates a significant division between the psychoanalytic listening stance, regardless of which channel is used, and pre-Freudian biological psychiatry. In fact, neuroleptic drugs are often used in an effort to quiet the patient down and put an end to bizarre and disruptive attempts at communication. The advantage of this form of treatment is that the patient appears less eccentric and is more acceptable in the community. But the disadvantage is that valuable efforts to communicate are discouraged. In the treatment of the psychotic patient, whether and how much to use various neuroleptic medication often becomes a crucial decision and depends primarily on whether the therapist is willing to undertake the long and arduous effort to develop a relationship with an individual who has been badly hurt and damaged and whose communication is therefore ambivalent, obscure, and carefully guarded. There is no question that intensive psychotherapy with the psychotic patient makes the greatest demands of all on our psychoanalytic listening skills as well as on our very personality. As Kahlbaum's patient Paul M. said, "When the principle has been disturbed, one's life is turned upside down."

LACAN INTERVIEWS A PSYCHOTIC PATIENT

To my knowledge, there is to date only one published verbatim English translation of the controversial psychoanalyst

Lacan interviewing a psychotic patient (Schneiderman 1980). This extremely valuable interview shows how the interviewer's theoretical preconceptions, as they are revealed in questions and responses to the patient's comments, decisively shape the course of the interview and determine the data presented. This influence of the therapist's preconceptions, as they are subtly communicated in the therapist's interventions, on the patient's responses poses one of the most difficult issues in the attempt to validate conclusions based on psychoanalytic listening.

Our best protection againt excessively shaping the patient's material is knowledge of our own theoretical preconceptions as well as of what is personally offensive and what is desirable to us. Some analysts claim that even the transference in the psychoanalysis of neurotic patients is decisively influenced by the analyst's listening stance and theoretical convictions (Black 1987). Psychotic patients are exquisitely sensitive and quickly pick up what we want to hear and even what sort of language we wish to engage in with them. They then will decide either to cooperate with us or to be utterly negativistic and even to present us with a caricature of ourselves, or to oscillate apprehensively between these extremes.

The Lacanian analytic cure seeks to unfold in reverse order the sequence of signifiers—the ever more disguised language in which the subject's desire has gradually been alienated. It interrogates the patient's signifiers and figures of speech, takes them literally, and seeks out the developmental order in which they appear. This order, as it appears in the patient's communications, is always regressive, from the most recent to the earliest. The Lacanian analysis then retraces their genesis. (For details on the Lacanian approach see, for example, Lemaire [1981] and Chessick [1985a, 1987a,b].)Remember that, like Kraeplin, Lacan is interviewing this patient before a group of psychiatrists and psychoanalysts.

> Lacan (Schneiderman 1980) said to the patient, "Tell me about yourself." The patient was silent. Lacan said, "I don't know why I would not let you speak. You know very well what is happening to you" (p. 19). The patient began, "I can't manage to get hold of myself."

This is a very unusual way to begin an interview with a psychotic patient, or with any patient, but it is typical of Lacan. The statement, "I don't know why I would not let you speak" in response to the patient's initial silence is steeped in Lacan's theoretical point of view regarding the Other of the analyst. One wonders how the patient would interpret it. It has almost the ambience of Rosen's (1953) *Direct Analysis*, in which the therapist takes an immediate omnipotent stance in relationship to the mute schizophrenic patient. As in the cases reported by Rosen, this seems to work, because the patient begins to speak with a remarkably interesting but ambiguous statement.

> Upon being asked to explain, the patient insisted that he was "disjointed in regard to language, disjunction between the dream and reality" (p. 19). He began to speak of the imaginary world and reality. He was unable to bring them together, a complaint clearly tailor-made for Lacan and which probably explains why the patient was chosen for the interview. The patient reported that certain speech imposes itself on his intellect, by which he means the rather typical complaint of schizophrenics that their thoughts or speech seems to come from outside of them or to be controlled by others, and he contrasts this kind of manipulation with his ordinary thinking. A central statement

> imposes itself on his brain: "You killed the bluebird. It's an anarchic system" (p. 20). The patient explained that such a sentence has no rational meaning and is imposed on his brain. When asked for other examples, he mentioned that he was aggressive, and Lacan interrupted by asking him what he meant by that. The patient responded, "I've explained." When Lacan countered that he did not appear to be aggressive, the patient stated that he was aggressive inside and could not say more. Lacan replied, "You are going to succeed in telling me how that happens" (p. 21).

Again, there is a strange omnipotent aura about Lacan's comment, and again, it seems to work.

> The patient went on to describe voices and telepathy causing him to hear aggressive sentences about political assassination and so forth. He claimed that he was diagnosed as having paranoid delusions, and Lacan noted that he turned toward one of the psychiatrists in the audience. Asking the patient about it, Lacan was told that the patient felt that that psychiatrist was mocking him. Lacan replied to the patient that this was surely not true.

Lacan's astuteness as a clinician manifests itself throughout this interview. His technique upon being presented with delusional material apparently is to directly confront and deny the validity of the delusion. This is consistent with his rather omnipotent approach to the patient.

> The patient described himself as the solitary center of a solitary circle, "a kind of god, the demiurge of a solitary circle, because this world is walled in, and I cannot make it pass into everyday reality. Everything which masturbates . . . [silence]" (p. 23). This was followed by his expressing

> anxiety about the interview with Lacan, whom he called "a well-known personality" and whom he had been afraid of meeting. The patient, with remarkable honesty, added that the listening audience oppressed him, making it difficult to speak and rendering him anxious and tired.

Thus he is appealing to Lacan to let up on the pressure, and he is asking for help.

> Again the astute clinician, Lacan shifted to asking about basic historical material, to questions aimed at gathering case information that would not evoke anxiety.

By seeing to it that the patient's anxiety is not allowed to get out of hand, Lacan demonstrates an important interviewing principle. When the patient begins to discuss his delusions and masturbation, Lacan gives him a chance to express his anxiety about the subject and then relieves him by shifting to less anxiety-laden material.

Lacan's approach to this problem is in contrast to that of Kahlbaum because Lacan, about one hundred years later, is clearly not anxious about the patient's masturbation and is more in tune with the patient's state. The interview should be studied for the gentle way in which Lacan leads the patient into revealing his anxiety about being interviewed and his sense of being oppressed by the group. It should be noted at this point that no particular channel of listening need predominate, because the main issue at the beginning of the interview is to make the patient sufficiently comfortable to produce communication at all—remember, he was mute at the beginning. The hope is that he will then go on to communicate feelings and material not related to his anxiety and discomfort at being interviewed. Whether this is possible in front of a group is highly questionable (Zinberg 1987).

How the Therapist's Preconceptions Shape the Transmission

> A little later, the patient began to speak of his nervous breakdown after a disappointment with a woman. He described his mother as very anxious and very silent: "The evening meal was very silent; there was no true affective contact from my mother. She was anxious, her mental state was contagious" (p. 25). His father came home on the weekends and this resulted in family fights and a tense, anxiety-provoking atmosphere. The patient concluded, "I think that by osmosis I myself was very anxious" (p. 25). Lacan interrupted to ask about osmosis and again brought in the issue of the real and the imaginary.

At this point, theoretical preconceptions determine Lacan's response. Although the patient is proceeding to speak of crucial family relationships, Lacan—in contrast, for example, to the focus of Sullivan or Laing (1969)—interrupts the flow of communication. He is clearly interested in his realms of the symbolic, the imaginary, and the real, and he is going to lead this patient into that sort of discussion. From the traditional psychoanalytic point of view, there would be little reason to intervene at this point.

The patient's use of *osmosis*, which Lacan, with his usual perspicacity, picked up, is discussed in the publications of Sullivan's (for example, 1947, 1953) superb work with schizophrenics. In Sullivan's writings (mostly transcribed lectures and seminars), much importance is attributed to the contagious nature of anxiety, which this patient is describing with respect to his home life. An interactive listening approach might therefore elicit a comment from the psychiatrist linking the patient's sense of anxiety with the interviewer and the anxiety that he felt at home in the presence of either his mother or his father. Here one might begin searching for the beginnings of a transference. The self psychologist would be concerned with further questions aimed at finding out how the patient relieved anxiety when he was living at home.

> The patient responded to Lacan's interruption by revealing some of his psychotic delusional material, about which he goes on at some length. Remarkably, he returned to his opening comment and discussed how he tried to get hold of himself in relation to what he conceived of as a curious body and mind hiatus in himself, with which he was obsessed. He concluded, "I tried, by poetic action, to find a balancing rhythm, a music. I was led to think that speech is the projection of an intelligence which arises toward the outside" (p. 26).

This is why the self-psychological approach has proven of such great clinical utility in understanding the communications of severely preoedipally disturbed patients. This patient, like Ellen West, is attempting to explain his fragmentation and to soothe himself with such activities as poetry and music. Ominously, his explanations are paranoid delusions, but one can almost observe his efforts to get hold of himself and put everything together into some kind of coherent form in order to relieve a profound discomfort. He had already described this discomfort when he voiced his concern about being the solitary center of a solitary circle—that is, his utter detachment from meaningful human relationships.

> Lacan went on at some length, drawing out this kind of confusing material about speech, images, and intelligence from the patient, but the discussion, perhaps because of Lacan's penetrating approach, slides gradually to the patient's sexual confusion and continuing anxiety about being interviewed. The patient reported the impression at

one time that he was going to become a woman. Lacan pressed him as to whether he actually felt himself to be a woman. Although Lacan pressed very hard, the patient was evasive and attributed seeing himself as a woman to an occurrence in a dream.

An argument ensued in which Lacan attempted to clarify the difference between waking dreams and night dreams and to understand where the patient's imposed speech intervened. Lacan then tried to decipher what the patient was signifying by the various quotations from his imposed speech, such as, "They want to kill me, the bluebirds" (p. 33). The patient explained that this phrase implied a world where he was without boundaries and at the same time confusingly presented the paradoxical state in which he lived in a solitary circle without boundaries. Lacan objected that a solitary circle does not imply living without boundaries since the individual is bounded by the solitary circle. The patient explained the paradox by pointing out that he lives simultaneously in a real and imaginary world. In the real world he lives with boundaries because of his body, but in the realm of the imaginary, in relation to the solitary circle, he lives without boundaries. Lacan's point was to show the patient that he, Lacan, floundered in the patient's system, that he cannot understand it. He wants the patient to explain "your world." The patient responded that he regards himself as a transmitting telepath, although only certain persons can receive the transmission of his thoughts. He does not think Lacan has received this transmission. Lacan astutely concluded that the questions he asked showed the patient that he was floundering and that was why the patient felt that he had not received the telepathic transmissions.

The patient then described these transmissions, which involved the feeling that he could be heard through the radio. He had the impression that someone was listening to

> him and making fun of him. He continued, "I was really at the end of my rope, because with this telepathy, which had been going on for a while, I had other neighbors who I had abused and who looked at me strangely. All of a sudden I wanted to commit suicide and I took . . ." [Lacan interrupts] (p. 37). The patient wanted suicide as an escape from anxiety.

Lacan is clearly enticed here by the patient's realms of psychic functioning involving the imaginary, reality, telepathy, and so on. He corners the patient by astute questioning in order to show the conflicting levels on which the patient exists, which he is clearly trying to demonstrate to the audience. An interactive listening stance would conclude that this patient is responding to Lacan's pressured questioning by revealing progressively more psychotic material. This reaction is common among schizophrenic patients who are being made increasingly anxious. Lacan does not pick up the theme of anxiety, which recurs again and again, or the theme of the patient's repeated but inept efforts to get hold of himself—which is really central to the material and at the core of his illness.

The traditional psychoanalytic viewpoint might view these central delusional themes as autistic and regressive, whereas a self psychologist would stress the patient's heroic effort to form some kind of a cohesive self experience. An object relations theorist would focus on the patient's feeling that the neighbors and others, including members of the audience to the interview, were making fun of him. This projection represents the patient's anger and his attempt to project split-off all-bad self and object representations onto the neighbors or the audience. There is clearly a confusion of ego boundaries represented by the patient's concern with living in a world with no boundaries and a confusion of who wants to kill whom—"dirty political assassinations"—with the bluebirds representing some kind of projected malevolent internalized object.

Phenomenologists would regard this encounter as unsatisfactory from a therapeutic point of view. Their evidence is found in the final clinical material. Of course this is to be expected, since Lacan is using this interview as a demonstration of his theories to other psychiatrists rather than as an attempt at a therapeutic encounter with the patient. So it is not surprising that the patient poignantly concludes:

> I have a hope, a hope of finding my power of judgment again, my power of dialogue, a power to get hold of the personality. I think that that is the most crucial problem. Like I had told you at the beginning, I can't manage to get hold of myself. [p. 40]

THE DANGER OF A SINGLE-CHANNEL APPROACH

Lacan, like Binswanger in the case of Ellen West, expresses despair about this patient and concludes the interview by predicting that the patient will successfully commit suicide. Lacan is not so much interested in this patient's anxieties and methods of dealing with them as he is with the following statement from the patient:

> There is a very simple language that I use in everyday life, and there is on the other hand a language which has an imaginative influence, where I disconnect the people around me from the real . . . My imagination creates another world, a world which would

> have a sense which is equivalent to the sense of the world that is called real, but which would be completely disjoined. [p. 22]

For this interesting patient, who at times imagines himself a reincarnation of Nietzsche or Artaud, the imposed sentences, "to the extent that they emerge sometimes to go and aggress a person," represent bridges between the imaginative world and the real world. The fact that the patient places himself at the center of his imaginative world, which he creates with speech, and that he recognizes his insignificance in the real world, and the role of these constructions in the patient's efforts to allay anxiety, are not the focus for Lacan of this interview, but it *is* the focus for the patient, who specifically complains of "a psychological tension created, anxiety in relation to the real, but carnal, that is to say, in relation to the body . . ." (pp. 25–26). And we know that the patient is concerned about turning into a woman. He cannot get hold of himself.

> Lacan, like the doctors in the case of Ellen West and of Paul M. (from Kahlbaum), ended the interview by asking to see samples of the patient's writings.

From a traditional psychoanalytic point of view, this patient, like Judge Schreber (Freud 1911), was showing profound anxieties centering around repressed homosexual impulses, and his efforts to deal with these anxieties were similar to those described by Freud in his study of the memoirs of Judge Schreber. From an object relations point of view, this case focuses on the persecutory nature of the patient's projections, which are inducing in the patient fears of being criticized, attacked, blamed, or omnipotently controlled. The patient's life centers on his relationship with the imagined set of persecutors who, in their telepathic communications, go into and out of him at will, and so projective identification poses a central preoccupation for him.

From the point of view of self psychology, the patient's critical problem is his need to get hold of himself and form some kind of cohesive sense of self out of the fragments of his shattered personality in order to reduce the anxiety concomitant with the disintegration of the nuclear self (Kohut 1971). This secondary or restitutive resurrection of the archaic self and archaic selfobjects occurs in a psychotic form.

The interactive point of view would stress the anxiety that arises from the patient's relationships in the real world and his attempt to develop an imaginary existence, of which he is the center, in order to withdraw from this profound interpersonal anxiety. The entire shape of the interview would be heard as a demonstration of this central problem.

The phenomenological approach would emphasize the patient's hope, not only to succeed in overcoming his anxiety, but, as he says to Lacan (Schneiderman 1980), "in finding a possibility for a dialogue" (p. 37)—a dialogue that could lead him to an authentic existence rather than a life in which he views himself as a reincarnation of someone else. All of these channels of listening yield valuable information about this patient's condition; none of them necessitate the conclusion that the patient is hopeless and is bound to commit suicide.

As in the case of Kraeplin, previously described by Laing (1960), "the construction we put on this behavior will, however, depend on the relationship we establish with the patient" (pp. 30–31), and this patient's material can be explained in a number of ways. Like Kraeplin's patient, Lacan's patient is tormented and desperate. As Laing points out, "He is objecting to being measured and tested. He wants to be heard" (p. 31).

FOUR

LISTENING TO THE BORDERLINE PATIENT

MANY PATIENTS BEHAVE in sessions, as generally in their lives, as if no one responded to them in infancy with any sort of empathy or "affect attunement" (Stern 1985). Either there was no psychological response at all to their needs, or there was a negative response. As one such patient said to me, "I could feel my mother freeze up and get tense when I went to her for a hug." They complain that life is empty. They are miserable and unhappy—and they often manage to inflict misery and unhappiness on everyone around them. The most difficult of these patients, especially if they frequently display unpleasant anger and poor impulse control, are often diagnosed as suffering from a borderline personality disorder. Others, "if they are quiet and withdrawn, are called schizoid, and if functioning competently but isolated, compulsive" (Basch 1987, p. 376). All these patients are struggling in various ways with a severely defective capacity for tension regulation.

Closely related to this group of patients are the narcissistic character disorders, whose problem, Basch says, is not the basic control of tension but a fragile sense of self, as a result of the failure during infancy of affect attunement from the parents. The differentiation of these two groups, it seems to me, rests on the degree and relative subtlety of parental failure, in turn a function of parental capacities and expectations interacting with innate and constitutional factors in the patient. In those instances of gross parental failure, the individual emerges with a fundamental and all-preoccupying impairment of internal structures for tension reduction. Where the failure has been more subtle, or more marked with only one parent, the capacity for tension reduction is better, and protection from further disappointment becomes the central issue. Concerning this latter group Basch (1987) writes, "We see in these patients an unconscious preoccupation with protecting themselves from experiencing needs for love, understanding, and validation that early experience has convinced them will be met only by disappointment and painful humiliation" (p. 378).

Basch attempts to present a unified understanding of how to proceed in psychotherapy with these groups of patients as well as with neurotic patients, but some of the discussants of his paper maintain that we have far too little data to assess what is the correct base for any unified theory. In addition, some of them are more favorably disposed than Basch to the dual-instinct theory, which, as Cooper points out, "in an odd way has been more accommodating than its adherents would acknowledge" (Basch 1987, p. 387), and they are not disposed to employ the concepts of self psychology.

Basch argues that Freud's dual-instinct theory "is not a psychoanalytic theory at all, but a speculation or hypothesis in the area of biology" (p. 369). He maintains that the brain is an information-processing organ and not an energy-discharging organ, but he adds that our therapeutic efforts are successful "when we are able to help the patient manage affective tensions more effectively than he was able to do before coming to see us" (p. 375).

One argument among proponents of the various listening stances centers on the acceptance or rejection of Greenberg's contention in his discussion of Basch's paper that "it is simply mistaken to assume that sexuality and aggression are primary irreducible forces motivating all human behavior" (Basch 1987, p. 392). Basch, of course, from the point of view of self psychology, would agree with this. Following Greenberg's erudite discussion once more, it becomes apparent that the various theories on which the listening stances are based are simply incompatible—although Greenberg labels this a "healthy incompatibility" (p. 397). Even within traditional psychoanalysis, as Cooper (1988) maintains, two descriptions of analytic activity as exemplified by the work of Strachey and Loewald, "the metapsychological description of goals, and the interactive and phenomenological description of process, are not readily translatable into each other; they are parallel rather than integrated" (p. 26).

Mitchell, the final discussant of Basch's paper, points out that there is no unstructured listening unmediated by theory, and that different theoretical models orient the analyst to "different kinds of deep structures which are felt to underlie the fabric of human experience" (Basch 1987, p. 401). From his point of view, all psychoanalytic models are "interpretive systems for arranging the experiential pieces of data of the analysand's life and the interactive data of the analytic relationship into a composition which imparts meaning and hopefully enriches, opens up previously closed-off possibilities" (Basch 1987, p. 402). Basch concludes by maintaining that his theory of psychology is rooted in the brain's complex need to order, and that competence and the resulting self-esteem are the experiential evidence that such order has been reached. In a later publication, Basch (1988) develops and illustrates his theory in detail.

THE CASE OF MISS BANKS

Let us turn now to the case of Miss Banks from Basch's (1980) *Doing Psychotherapy*. She was a 27-year-old graduate student in social psychology who had had previous psychotherapy and who applied for further treatment when she transferred to a local university.

> The therapist asked what had brought Miss Banks to the clinic. She officiously replied that she had been in therapy for three years and had "an unresolved Oedipus complex." She maintained that she and her previous therapist had decided that her mother was depressed and that her father had preferred her to her mother because she was the entertaining, intelligent companion that he had always wanted. She claimed that this made it impossible for her to form lasting and meaningful heterosexual relationships, but she added that although she now understood what was wrong with her, she was still unable to find a suitable

> partner. She immediately went on to say that the new therapist looked young and that perhaps she needed a female therapist.

Basch points out that the patient is not approaching the new therapist as an authority, rather, she presents herself as a sophisticated patient ready to challenge a beginner. Why does she do this? Using the drive/conflict/defense orientation, we hear an immediate hostility to a male authority figure and the beginning of some depreciation or castration of him. An object relations stance might borrow from Klein and emphasize the patient's need to devalue the therapist, scoop out his knowledge, and enhance her own self-esteem at his expense.

The phenomenology of the encounter is already unpleasant, and the patient clearly relates, at least to male authority figures, in a way that has a distancing effect. The interactionist would stress the fact that the therapist is young and is probably in training, so that there is a core of truth to the patient's concern; it is not simply "transference." The interactionist might add that, considering the patient's educational background, it would not be surprising that she might think that if one's first therapist is a male, then one's next therapist ought to be a female.

Basch cleverly provides a series of imagined vignettes between the therapist and Miss Banks in which the two of them could easily become entangled in a confrontational and hostile exchange, sometimes with the patient stalking out of the room angrily and slamming the door behind her. Patients who behave in such a manner are, of course, frequently labeled borderline. Basch uses the self-psychological stance. He formulates the provisional hypothesis that the patient antagonizes men who might be interested in her, but that she is unaware that she is doing so.

> Picking up on the theme of the patient's statement that she cannot find a suitable partner, the therapist asked her whether there was a man in her life now. The patient responded by describing one man whom she had never dated and another man, Bill, with whom she had broken up after two months. Actually, she said, she had transferred to the local university because it was an hour or so away from her parents, enabling her to go home on the weekends. She had often fought with Bill, and she insisted that men don't want a woman who competes with them. The session ended with the patient's asking challenging questions and complaining that the therapist had said nothing signficant, but she left without rage, agreeing somewhat casually to return.

This interview offers a superb example of how a patient who could easily end up being labeled borderline can, if listened to properly, be worked with in psychotherapy. The first step required the therapist to move away from his anger and try to understand the patient's provocativeness as part of a character pattern or, more formally, a defense transference. Because he was able to do this, he was able to get the patient to report further episodes from her life history of similar behavior. Although the interview was left unresolved, the patient at least seemed willing to return. This would have to be the goal no matter which stance was employed, and at this point any interpretation based on any theoretical model would have been bait for the patient to initiate a provocative exchange and an angry disruption.

> The second session began with further doubts on the patient's part and further provocation. The therapist was remarkably tolerant of the patient's argumentative behavior, which he was then able to relate to her difficulty in

> starting with a new therapist, and he noted her resentment at having to transfer from the previous therapist. She now sounded sad and resigned.

Again the therapist's capacity to remain thoughtful and reasonable in the face of the patient's provocativeness apparently enabled her to come forward with what was troubling her at the moment—namely, the loss of her former therapist.

> It turned out that the former therapist had gone into private practice and the patient could not afford to go with him. She now abruptly exploded in the session when she was asked to tell the new therapist what happened. She left screaming and slammed the door.

This outburst of emotion, as Basch points out, is clearly related to the strength of the patient's feelings about the disruption of her previous therapy, and the label "borderline" is suggested by her poor control over her emotional impulses. However, Basch points out that this diagnosis is often a sign that the therapist has been made angry and unsatisfied "by a patient who will not play the game by the rules and leaves the therapist at a loss as to what to do next to make therapy effective" (p. 60).

> The therapist decided neither to diagnose Miss Banks's behavior as borderline nor to make any effort to contact her, for example, in order to shore up her defenses against inner turmoil. He chose to do nothing except to wait for the patient's next move, especially since she had left her sunglasses behind when she stamped out of the office.

Any therapist might judge this patient to be suffering from a borderline personality disorder, as she already shows many of the characteristics of this diagnosis as described in the DSM-IIIR. The real issue is not one of diagnosis, but one of whether to take an analytic stance toward this patient or a supportive-psychotherapy stance. The answer depends not on the diagnosis, but on the communications that are received from the patient depending on which listening stance is used. It is not uncommon at the beginning of psychotherapy for patients to show their worst side first. This is because they are very anxious and upset; they have to begin with a stranger, and, as in the case of Miss Banks, there may have been a disruption of a previous therapy or there may have been other life experiences that pressured them into unwillingly placing themselves in a situation in which there is again a chance of developing intimacy with a stranger.

Diagnoses, such as borderline personality disorder or even schizophrenia, are often made early in the therapy on the basis of the relatively poor ego functioning demonstrated by temporarily extremely anxious or enraged patients. A more suitable strategy, regardless of which listening stance is used, is to be open-minded about diagnosis for a number of sessions in the hope that the patient quiets down and becomes comfortable with the new procedure, which for the patient may seem strange and unprecedented. This usually does happen, although in a small percentage of cases emergency interpretations must be made quite early, especially if there is massive distortion of reality testing or what Kernberg (1975) might call the disruptive early projection of "all-bad" self and object representations onto the therapist. Although there is some evidence of this sort of projection at the beginning in this case, it is by no means clear, and the therapist was well advised to wait for at least a while before intervening with interpretations.

> The patient appeared for the next treatment session, and the therapist encouraged her to talk about the parting with her previous therapist. The patient reported that she had been one of his first patients when he was in training. At the end of his training when he decided to go into private practice, he urged her to approach her father for money to pay for the treatment. The patient refused to do this because her father did not believe in therapy and she had never told him that she was seeing a psychiatrist. She insisted to the first therapist that "he owed it to me as a patient to continue on the same financial basis as before" (p. 63). Her argument was that he had used her to get through his training and he had never paid her for that. The first therapist became enraged, which was quite atypical from his usual behavior toward her. This episode led to the termination of their relationship.
>
> The present therapist interpreted the patient's argument about money as a "camouflage" of her fear of telling her father that she was in treatment and asking him to pay for it. The patient neither agreed nor strongly disagreed with this interpretation, but she conceded that her father had a terrible temper and she was frightened of what he might do. She added that she has a brother three years younger than she who was born retarded and that her father blamed it on her mother's family. The patient's mother's depression seemed to be related to having to institutionalize this retarded child and feeling that she was to blame for his birth.

This therapist is clearly and effectively using the self-psychological approach. He is attempting to establish an atmosphere of tolerance to her overreactions and difficulty with tension reduction in the interest of drawing her out and encouraging her to connect her emotionally unstable states with specific life historical incidents. This is the self-psychological approach at its best in dealing with explosive, unstable, or borderline patients. The interpretation offered is only a partial one, meant primarily to help the patient to a better understanding of her outbursts rather than to focus on the transference. Note how different this technique is from "confronting" the patient with her alleged projections and distorted reality testing.

> The fourth session opened with Miss Banks talking about "the Oedipus business," in which she recapitulated the rather stereotyped interpretations of her "Oedipus complex" from the previous therapy. The therapist avoided comment and urged the patient to go ahead and discuss what was on her mind. It turned out she was worried that the problem she had with the previous therapist would arise again with him when he enters into private practice. He admitted that he would be doing so in eight months, thus, in a sense, setting a time limit on the therapy; the patient responded by crying. The patient protested that she could not establish a therapeutic alliance or have any idea of what kind of a person the therapist might be in such a short period. The therapist replied that he understood thus far that she was frightened, and said that he hoped to talk about that with her.

Basch objects to the assumption that psychotherapeutic results based on insight can be achieved only over a period of many years. He does not discuss the effect of setting an advance time limit on an insight-oriented therapy. Freud (1918b), in the case of the Wolf Man, unwittingly showed that when a definitive date for the end of therapy is set, it tends to drive deeper material underground and encourage a massive identification with the therapist, who in a sense then becomes vital to the integrity of the patient's psychic structure. It was only when the Wolf Man later heard that Freud had developed cancer and might die that he broke down once more. Similarly with this patient, from an interactive point of view, the definitive setting of a date to end the therapy carries the risk of encouraging a massive identification with the therapist and driving deeper material underground. However this case of Miss Banks is an uncovering psychotherapy, not a psychoanalysis, so the result hoped for in health and autonomy would not be as extensive. Identification with the therapist could shore up her wobbly ego functioning.

From a phenomenological point of view, one might argue that the therapist's manifest tolerance is a function of the fact that he knows he is only going to be working with this unpleasant patient for eight months. He also must protect himself from the anticipated pain of a forthcoming separation with this patient by limiting his "presence" rather carefully. An interactive point of view might stress the dramatic impact on this patient of this sudden announcement of impending separation, just after she is beginning to open up about her father and has disclosed that she never knows what to expect from him.

> Indeed, the patient then continued about her father and his explosive loss of temper. At one point she introduced this subject by reporting a fear that the therapist would lose his temper and get angry at her for nothing and would not understand that she was trying her best.

This seems to be a possible reference to the therapist's announcement that they will have to terminate in eight months; yet the therapist sees no reason for her to be afraid of an explosion on his part. Her fear becomes connected with her explosive father, but this therapist does not make much of the previous therapist's sudden angry behavior, as a therapist with an interactive approach might do. From the self-psychology point of view, the purpose here is to get an empathic grasp of how the patient felt in response to parental failure. But Langs (1982) might label it a collusion to avoid the patient's raging reaction to the therapist's introducing a termination date. His listening stance represents an extreme interactive view. The possibility of projection in this material is not discussed, and the patient is steered toward a discussion of her parents.

> As the patient reported unpleasant incidents involving herself and her parents, the therapist developed sympathy "with the little girl who meant well and got yelled at" and "no longer has to remind himself not to take personally the patient's mistrust and anger" (p. 68).

What appears here is the beginning of transference and countertransference. But it would be heard differently on different channels of listening, depending on the emphasis placed on the therapist's surprise announcement to the patient that he would be leaving in eight months.

> The fifth session was taken up with a discussion, encouraged by the therapist, of the patient's childhood. She talked at some length about the many unhappy incidents that had marked her early life. The therapist offered few interpretations.

The therapist picked up the patient's need for praise in the developing relationship in which he was the teacher and she was the pupil hoping for his reassurance. The therapist formed a hypothesis in subsequent sessions that the patient's life was devoid of opportunities to enhance her self-esteem by pleasing others and that her parents were too unhappy to be able to be gratified by her accomplishments. The therapist was inclined to reassure her of his interest when she doubted it, and he generally provided mirroring interventions. For example, when the patient was given advanced responsibilities on the job, the therapist did not hesitate to show pleasure and to congratulate her. At the same time, his hope was to uncover her problems and help her gain insight into her characteristic behavior patterns rather than simply suppport her pathological defenses.

As the case of Miss Banks unfolds, the ambience, reassurance, and acceptance offered by the therapist lead to the establishment of a vital selfobject transference, which was not essentially interpreted or resolved in the therapy. In treating such patients, says Basch, rather than "working toward getting the patient to like him, the therapist needs to work toward being able to like himself as he is functioning with a particular patient in a particular session . . . failure to be satisfied with himself is a clear signal that something is amiss" (p. 75). This is an extremely valuable method of listening to one's self for countertransference.

> As termination was being considered, Miss Banks decided to become a physician like her father and began to devote herself to this goal; a year later she called the therapist to tell him that she had been accepted to a medical school and felt content with her life at that point.

Basch insists that her decision to become a physician does not represent an unresolved transference—an identification with both her physician father and the physician therapist—or "an attempt to resolve a neurotic conflict through action rather than through psychological insight" (p. 86), because she proceeded with her plans in a thoughtful fashion, was not "driven," and achieved genuine satisfaction from the process.

The Centrality of the Patient's Oedipus Complex

> For a brief time the patient sexualized the transference and became frightened by her sexual thoughts. The therapist pointed out that she was mistakenly attributing genital motives to the love and affection she felt for him. The cause of this love and affection was that, through his work, he was giving her a chance to achieve satisfaction that she could not have had before. "She was helped to understand that her emotions were appropriate to the child who stands in awe of and wants to unite with the powerful, giving parent, and were not those of a sexually excited woman" (p. 86).

The issue of whether or not Basch offered an "inexact interpretation" that led to the events around termination of the therapy is a controversial one, fraught with the difficulty of various interpretations of reported psychoanalytic data. Such an argument cannot be resolved here and tends to obscure Basch's main point: If the patient is judged to be suffering from a disorder of the self or a narcissistic disorder, the therapeutic work ought to focus on threatened fragmentations, disruptions, and temper tantrums that occur upon disappointment in the archaic selfobject—phenomena that prevent the patient from having successful interpersonal experiences or being able to form an affective, empathic, selfobject matrix.

Sexualization is met with muted treatment in this approach and is not interpreted as a representation of infantile lust or aggression; the focus is on the patient's need for mirroring or idealizing selfobjects. If the therapist has judged wrongly, or if the narcissistic phenomena are predominantly defensive regressions from an unresolved Oedipus complex, therapy, according to the critics of self psychology, will represent a collusion between patient and therapist to avoid the emergence of infantile aggressive and sexual issues (both homosexual and heterosexual). Clinical judgment is involved here, and in making this judgment the reader should keep in mind that the therapy lasted only eight months, as announced in advance.

Curtis (1985) points out that the therapist in this case did not seem especially concerned about whether genital sexuality would ever play a part in the life of this patient, and he complains that "in view of her major difficulty in her relationship with men and the significant conflict about her father, it is difficult to understand how the erotic transference can be so easily dismissed" (p. 355). Here we have an irreconcilable difference in channels of listening. Curtis believes that the patient was "apparently only too glad" to accept the therapist's denial of her sexual interest in him and to turn her attention to achievements and nonsexual interests. He severely criticizes the therapist's statement that the patient's feelings were not those of a sexually excited woman and maintains that "in so doing, he was indeed enacting the role of the powerful parent forcing her, in collusion with her own resistance to her sexual urges, to renounce sexuality and, like a good latency child, 'single-mindedly' attend to her studies" (p. 355).

Curtis claims that this is indeed an inexact interpretation, offering a new displacement or compromise formation in order to relieve anxiety and symptoms. Thus listening on one channel may lead to interpretations that are then described, if one listens on another channel, as inexact and leading only to compromise formations. The fundamental flaw claimed here by Curtis is that the wrong channel of listening was used. This is an irreconcilable argument. Curtis, using the drive/conflict/defense orientation, strongly proposes that this patient's narcissistic defenses concealed conflicts in relationships with men that could very well have been interpreted and understood along the lines of the Oedipus complex, regardless of the quality of the patient's first therapy, which seemed to be largely intellectual.

Waldron (1983) claims that Basch used the concepts of self psychological theory to avoid exploration of the patient's sexual conflicts. He considers Basch's comment that the achievement of full genital object love is not the therapist's concern to be an "astounding conclusion." What Basch actually says is that whether the patient "will eventually marry, and whether genital sexuality will play an important part in her life . . . are questions that need not be the concern of the therapist" (p. 86). The point is again made by Waldron that using the listening channel of self psychology tends to focus the therapist on problems of the self and on preoedipal issues. It lends itself to an avoidance of underlying nuclear oedipal conflicts. On the other hand, critical reviewers of Basch's book have not sufficiently emphasized his demonstrated generation, while working from the point of view of self psychology, of a therapeutic ambience that is comfortable and supportive, an ambience that is of special importance in the intensive psychotherapy of explosive borderline patients.

THE CASE OF MAE

In a previous publication, I presented a detailed case report of the long-term intensive psychotherapy of a borderline patient (Chessick 1982b). The case raises questions similar to those raised by Basch's case about the value of interpretations in the early phases of therapy with such patients, regardless of which theories are chosen as the basis of these interpretations. Stress was placed on (1) the value of attunement to the patient, (2) the importance of staying with the patient through the many vicissitudes of long-term treatment, and (3) the patient's reparative use of a long treatment, in which she relived certain phases of her development in the transference. Acquisition of internalized controls may need to occur in this way before the patient is even ready to use interpretations. This patient forced me to open new channels for listening to borderline patients. She remained in a sitting up face-to-face position during the twice-weekly sessions, which continued through a number of years.

> Mae began the first session by reporting a nightmare in which "grandpa was being nice to me but I tried to cross the street away from him. He cut me in the back with a razor." The first six months of therapy were marked by a flood of rageful dreams that revolved around humiliation by men and devaluation of men. The earliest interpretive attempts based on such material were intended to call the patient's attention to her splitting of object representations into all good and all bad, perceiving the latter, usually represented as male authorities, to be treacherous, dangerous, and assaultive. Her response to such interpretations was consistent: rage and a sense of profound insult and narcissistic wounding. Nevertheless, the patient continued to attend sessions regularly.

If the interpretations from this framework of object relations were not accurate, well timed, or properly phrased, or if they were simply ill-advised and wrong, then the patient's reaction would be explained. But another possibility is that this borderline patient was not yet ready for any interpretations.

> I later shifted the interpretive stance to identifying her intense narcissistic sensitivity, her need to be omnipotent and to control the therapist entirely, and her assigning me the role of a soothing selfobject. I noted, for example, her rage and feelings of having been insulted when I went on vacation or when sessions were over. Here again, the patient made no apparent response to this interpretive work, behaving in her personal life as she had before, although she was less enraged by this sort of interpretation.

Subject to the aforementioned reservations, it again seemed possible that the patient was not ready for any interpretations. She could neither use nor integrate them; perhaps she could not even hear them. In this sense, any interpretive attempt represented an empathic failure, a failure to understand what she was struggling with. All interpretations were met with rage, at worst, and indifference at best. Finally, using a drive/conflict/defense orientation and the structural theory, I heard material that suggested that the patient's ego was preoccupied in the therapy with the discharge of rage and fantasies of revenge, so as to reduce internal pressure and to enable continued functioning outside the therapeutic situation. The patient's ego was struggling valiantly to deflect and contain this explosive affect. Also, she at least temporarily needed pacification and unification (Gedo and Goldberg 1973) and help with adaptive skills.

> I attempted to explore with the patient specific instances in which minor narcissistic wounds threw her into a towering rage and to accumulate evidence for her of her incredible sensitivity, gross exaggerations, and paranoid feelings as pathological ways of dealing with this overwhelming rage.

The therapist here functions as an accessory ego, helping her to learn calming down and self-observation. It seemed that the patient's ego and self state were in need of constant support, unification, and repair through a consistent relationship before she could bear the additional burden of deeper exploration. Indeed she offered little choice: With all her raging, the atmosphere was not conducive to reflection about anything.

This patient was instructive, as was Miss F. in Kohut's (1971) early work, essentially teaching me about her needs. By listening on all the channels, one can eventually tune in to patients' communications as a guide to how they are to be approached at any given time in interpretive work. If one adheres rigidly to any given listening stance, this vital guidance may be missed; an impasse results, accompanied by an explosion of rage and disappointment in which the patient is labeled borderline.

> My most important contribution in the first year of the patient's treatment was to work calmly and with minimal anxiety, trying to understand the patient's material without being sucked into the stormy chaos. At the deepest level, my main contribution may have been in not being destroyed by the patient's raging. At the end of the first year of therapy the patient dreamed "my father was urging me to do a forward flip and I agreed to do it." Her associations were that the "forward flip" was "hopeful" and it was certainly different from her usual rage-and-destruction dreams.

WHAT TO LISTEN FOR FROM BORDERLINE PATIENTS

The central problem in the treatment of borderline patients is that of dealing with their inevitable disruptive rage. Even in the case reported by Basch, the patient stormed out of the second session, leaving the therapist confused as to what to do next. In the case reported by Basch, it turned out best that he did nothing but wait for the next session; but sometimes there is not a scheduled next session, and the patient must be contacted. It is especially for this type of patient that Schwaber's recommendations for psychoanalytic listening, reviewed in Chapter 1, are most important. In order to deal with such explosions of rage, one must make every effort to put oneself empathically in the shoes of the patient in order to understand how the patient is experiencing the therapy, despite our best efforts and good intentions. Here the interactive channel is often the most helpful because the patient experiences our mistakes in therapy as inexcusable shortcomings and failings, and responds as if insulted. Underlying this, of course, is the narcissistic sense of entitlement to perfect empathy and understanding, but our knowing that is irrelevant to the immediate vicissitudes of the treatment.

I remain convinced that meticulous attention to the details of the interaction is the best starting point in dealing with patients such as those suffering from paranoid or borderline personality disorders, who are subject to explosions of rage in the treatment. What is important is not the therapist's minor empathic failures per se, but the way in which they are experienced by the patient. The patient uses these minor empathic failures to relive a dreadful interpersonal experience in a protective effort to further demonstrate the need for distancing in interpersonal relationships. What we are listening for is how the patient is experiencing the interaction with the therapist and in what context these experiences are being placed within the patient's preexisting patterns. It is only after we have been able to establish this information that we can begin asking why these experiences are placed in a particular context.

Mae had been presented in childhood with the dilemma, which seemed all too real to her at the time, that a close, warm, sexual relationship would be accompanied by her literal physical destruction. Reawakening deep symbiotic longings meant disintegration of her fragile psychic structure and balance, a regression back to the infantile experience of depletion and utter lack of stimulation, a psychic death. This patient's pathology was so overwhelming that no one, in contrast to the case presented by Basch, could argue that she was regressively retreating from a central Oedipus complex.

> At an early point in the treatment, as Mae began to realize that no massive "feeding" (her term) or magical maternal giving was going to come from me, the relationship became very stormy and she began to search for ways to frighten and threaten me. She began to speak of suicide or of killing my family. Finally, she resolved the problem by not caring what I said; nothing made sense to her except the soothing sound of my voice. Interpretations and comments had not the slightest effect on this; the sound of my voice was her focus, and she stared at me for long periods.

This represents the limiting point as to whether a given borderline patient is treatable by psychoanalytically oriented psychotherapy: If the patient can somehow find a way to use the therapy and to tolerate the massive rage and frustration that is engendered because the therapist cannot possibly fulfill the enormous archaic selfobject needs, the therapy can proceed and structure building can slowly take place. There are some patients who simply cannot tolerate the neediness that is evoked by the therapeutic situation itself or the humiliation that is involved in being a patient at all. Others can never get over their paranoid suspiciousness, so they reach a certain level of distance in the relationship and remain indefinitely on a plateau. These are the patients who are often diagnosed as having a severe structural defect or a "psychotic core," and their cases do not usually give rise to arguments about whether there is a hidden nuclear Oedipus complex.

These are also the patients who are best listened to along all channels in order to find the most effective way of relating to them; they will often guide us by their responses to the different interventions we have made depending on which theoretical listening stance we have been using. With these very difficult patients, we can sometimes reach a favorable match by experimenting with various stances, so that the patient is eventually able to tolerate the therapy without so much disruption and explosion. Whether this represents simply finding the inexact interpretation that is most comfortable for the patient or whether it represents a genuine understanding of the patient's feelings at a given time remains almost impossible to determine at that time, but later, as the patient's narrative unfolds, the answer to this question becomes clarified.

Actually, the patient gives us no choice. If we stay rigidly with one theoretical stance, the patient will leave the therapy in a rage, will lead us to an impasse, or will become compliant so that all the important material is driven underground while the patient identifies with the aggressor analyst. There are often plenty of signals that this sort of process is taking place; Kohut (1984), in his discussion of the shortcomings of certain training psychoanalyses, discusses the latter outcome at some length.

THE CASE OF LOUISA A.

In an outstanding paper, Tolpin (1983) presents a similar therapeutic problem, attempting to illustrate Kohut's contention that primary deficits and persisting needs in psychological development enter into and form specific transference-like phenomena in the course of treatment. These needs have been largely repressed, disavowed, or discharged in a variety of symptoms and behaviors that often get the patient labeled borderline. In the case of Louisa A., "an attractive, intelligent, divorced woman in her early forties" (p. 461), Tolpin points out how the attempt at psychoanalysis stirred up the patient's unconscious primary needs, which had previously been manifested in kleptomania, bulimia, sexualization, and drug use.

> The problem presented by the therapy was that without the sense that her analyst could be always available to succeed in understanding and explaining the meaning of these needs, "the patient would have no choice but to go hungry, as it were, or to retreat again behind a complex and overdetermined defensive facade" (p. 480). Tolpin was the patient's fourth therapist. Each previous treatment had lasted less than a year; the first and third were terminated when the therapist moved to another city, and the second therapist developed a rapidly progressive disease and died. Tolpin carefully describes the patient's tragic background and multiple symptomatology. She had been a neglected, lonely child, especially after her father died when she was 9 years old.

> She began once-weekly treatment, but after four months she requested to be in analysis, which was planned to begin when Tolpin returned from vacation. A very intense erotized positive transference developed, based around the issue of the therapist's reliability. When the therapist went on vacation, the patient fragmented, seeking recourse in drugs and other acting-out behavior. Although she had little previous interest in serious music, the patient bought the late Beethoven quartets and played them frequently while the therapist was on vacation. The therapist reported that he had spoken of these quartets "in passing some time before the summer vacation" (p. 468). He added, "The context of, or the reason for, my remarks about the quartets is not of particular importance here" (p. 468).

This judgment, which leaves the reader hanging in midair, is followed by the report of a dream in which the patient's boss is "examining her in a careful impersonal way, like a doctor, but then he began touching her erotically" (p. 468). One can only speculate about the connection between the therapist's remarks about the Beethoven quartets, the patient's purchase of these quartets, and this dream. Each channel of listening would produce a different speculation.

> The Beethoven quartets became quite significant in the therapy, especially Opus 130. "She wore out two records of Opus 130. She put it on tape so it would always be available" (p. 471). The therapist concluded that the gradual alteration of the patient's use of the late Beethoven quartet began with its function as a substitute for the idealized analyst's voice, comments, and presence. It was a transitional object that eventually became internalized. At one point the patient said, "It's an outside thing but it's an inside thing" (p. 472). Tolpin claimed that this gradual

> alteration represented changes in the self, a repair of structural deficits making Louisa A. "increasingly able to make reliable her own sense of worth, relatively independent of formerly needed selfobjects" (p. 482).

This case illustrates another end point in the treatment of patients with structural deficits. The patient's innovative use of the Beethoven quartet as described by Tolpin is fascinating and reveals an inner capacity on the part of the patient to find a way to internalize the empathic analyst and thereby raise her self-esteem. The limiting factor in therapy with such patients rests on their capacity to perform this internalization. Not all patients retain the capacity for transmuting internalization, even in a well-conducted psychotherapy using self psychology.

Listening on all the channels, we must try to detect signs that this internalization is taking place and, conversely, seek evidence that it is not taking place and try to understand why. In my experience, it sometimes begins to take place and then suddenly stops, and nothing seems to help the patient resume the process. Great patience and very careful listening are necessary in these situations, for sometimes the patient is reacting to a countertransference structure (Tower 1956) that has formed in the therapist and is unconsciously producing a deidealization of the therapist.

At other times, idealization and internalization of the therapist seems to be interfered with by the patient's need to cling "loyally" to family members. Somehow, or sometimes due to cultural factors, the patient experiences the internalization of the therapist as an act of disloyalty to spouse or parents. The patient feels uncomfortable and conflicted as he or she becomes aware of the increasing internalization of the idealized analyst. At other times a family member notices the change and jealously criticizes the patient for it, increasing the guilt.

Limitations to Psychoanalytic Listening

> The therapist noted that "although this highly focused transference experience has not yet evolved into an optimally reliable self-sustaining inner resource, it appears to be moving in that direction" (p. 479). He believed that it was primarily the idealizing father transference that allowed these changes to take place.

A variety of needs were "funnelled into an idealizing mode" (p. 481). From Tolpin's self-psychology channel, he explains the improvement as based on a "firming selfobject experience that would make up for the weakness of her nuclear self" (p. 481). The oedipal aspects of the transference are not interpreted.

> The patient wrote Tolpin that she now enjoys the Beethoven quartet Opus 130 along with a new male friend, and that "the extra-musical qualities are now within me and the music is . . . music" (p. 482).

One cannot help wondering, using the drive/defense/conflict model as we did earlier with my patient, whether Tolpin's patient has not used the therapy to enable her ego to work through her mourning over the sudden death of her father when she was 9 years old (and perhaps the loss of three prior therapists), on a background of the sudden loss of a beloved governess when she was 2 years old. As the patient herself reported, the death of her second therapist "epitomized all the losses she had suffered. She becomes attached to someone and then something happens to them and she loses them . . ." (p. 466).

Father and daughter were extremely close, although his time with her was controlled and limited. Consistent with Kohut's (1971) principle of "the vulnerability of new structures" (p. 44), a severe disppointment in early latency (her father's sudden death) could have destroyed the emergent resolution of her Oedipus complex and thrown her backward to a search for the idealized paternal selfobject. Narcissistic rage appears as each new such hopeful idealization is disappointed. Tolpin was sufficiently impressed with her and was stable and mature enough for her to resume her developmental phases and perhaps repair old losses by reliving her experiences with a significant parental figure in a much more favorable way.

> A recurrent transference theme began with an early dream of an initially empty marble chair, which in later dreams and fantasies was transformed into a comfortable chair. The patient and the father-analyst, with "enough time," sit close together in the chair, reading.

An object relations approach would concentrate on the use of the Beethoven quartet as a transitional object, enabling separation-individuation as the traumatic loss of the father, and earlier, of the governess, was worked through. A phenomenological channel would hear an example of an I–thou encounter in which the patient has moved from alienation to intimacy. An interactive approach might stress Tolpin's behavior as a good father, along with his unspecified remarks, such as those about the Beethoven quartets, in which he revealed something about himself "related to my openness about something she understood me to have a positive personal interest in" (p. 468), as setting the stage for this kind of father transference and enabling the patient to come to terms symbolically with her oedipal strivings. Thus she ends up listening to the music with an adult man, "a new male friend" (p. 482), and accomplishes the transition from the Oedipus complex to mature heterosexuality, a transition which was interrupted when her father died.

The central deficit in borderline patients rests on their poor self-image and resultant poor self-esteem. Contributions to the formation of this degraded self-image may be found by listening on every channel, for they are usually multiply determined by a variety of interpersonal and cultural factors as well as by a continuing downward spiral of disappointing experiences in interpersonal relationships. Such patients are the most difficult to work with because they stir up totalistic countertransferences (Kernberg 1976), which often lead to further disappointing interpersonal experiences. So an additional limiting capacity in the treatment of borderline patients lies in the therapist's ability to step away from the countertransference rage and hatred often engendered by such patients.

The first move in the direction of detaching from destructive countertransference is psychoanalytic listening. Hunt and Issacharoff (1977) review Racker's work on countertransference and remind us, using the object relations model, that there are two main categories of countertransference. They are based on (1) concordant identifications or empathy, which give us information about the patient's self experience, and (2) complementary identifications, which tend to make the therapist act and feel as if the patient's internalized objects are those of the therapist, evoking the therapist's neurotic remnants (see Chapter 3). Complementary identification gives us information about the patient's original objects, if we can only step away from the countertransference emotions that are engendered in us when such a revival of our residual neurotic difficulties takes place. In Chapter 3, I discussed the fact that extreme countertransference can lead to dangerous acting out under the pressure of projective identification from borderline and psychotic patients.

As Goldberg (1988) points out, the analyst always affects the patient in a most intricate and subtle interplay, "both through the analyst's presence as well as through the analyst's particular ways of attending to and organizing the clinical data" (p. xiii).

FIVE

LISTENING TO THE NEUROTIC PATIENT

ON OCTOBER 1, 1907, a 29-year-old man, suffering from aggressive impulses and fantasies, began an eleven-month treatment with Freud. He is described by Freud as a "youngish man of university education" suffering from (1) fears—that something may happen to his father (even though his father had been dead for nine years) and to a lady he admires; (2) compulsions—such as impulses to cut his throat with a razor; and (3) prohibitions—some of which were against ridiculous or unimportant things, and which were often connected so as to make it impossible to comply with all of them.

Freud reported on the progress of the case a number of times to his Wednesday evening group. In April 1908, while the case was in progress, he delivered a four- or five-hour report to the First International Psychoanalytic Congress (Jones 1955, p. 42). The published report of the case (Freud 1909), "Notes upon a Case of Obsessional Neurosis," appears in the *Standard Edition*, along with some notes preserved from the original sessions. The case has generally, and unfortunately, become known as that of the Rat Man, but, following Lipton (1977a), we will use Freud's pseudonym "Paul Lorenz." Freud reported that the eleven-month treatment was successful, but he adds in a footnote that the patient was later killed in World War I.

OVERVIEW OF THE CASE

Freud first saw the prospective patient sitting up in his study. The next day, the patient, now on the couch, began by reporting his sudden rejection, when he was 14 or 15, by a 19-year-old student friend, an event which he considered to be the first great blow of his life. Without transition and without questions from Freud, he launched immediately into a description of his sexual life, including scenes of creeping under his governess's skirt, watching another governess express abscesses on her buttocks, and sexual playing with governesses. Even in childhood he had dealt with this sexual experience in a neurotic way: He was tormented by the feeling that his parents knew his thoughts and that his father might die if he thought about such things as wishing to see girls naked.

In the second session, Paul Lorenz presented the famous rat-torture story told to him by the cruel captain. Freud writes that while telling this story,

> His face took on a very strange composite expression. I could only interpret it as one of *horror at pleasure of his own of which he himself*

> *was unaware.* He proceeded with the greatest difficulty: "At that moment the idea flashed through my mind *that this was happening to a person who was very dear to me.*" [pp. 166–167]

The persons very dear to the patient were the lady he admired and his father. Then the idea occurred to him that unless he repaid the captain and the lieutenant, this thought of the rat torture being applied to his father and his loved one would come true. He then presented a long, obscure, detailed story about money that had to be paid. The third session was filled with a description of his ambivalent efforts at fulfilling his obsesssional vow.

The patient occupied his fourth session by describing his father's death, nine years before, at which he was not present. When his aunt died, eighteen months after his father's death, the patient began to experience intense self-reproach, which Freud spent the sixth session trying to explain to the patient. In the seventh session the patient admitted his intense ambivalence about his father: He realized that his father's death and the inheritance he would receive might enable him to marry the lady he admired.

Freud then launches into a discussion of some obsessional ideas and their explanation, including the famous example of how, on the day of the departure of his ambivalently loved lady, the patient felt obliged to remove a stone from the road; the idea had struck him that her carriage would be driving on the same road in a few hours' time and might come to grief against this stone. A few minutes later it occurred to him that this idea was absurd—and he was obliged to go back and replace the stone in its original position in the middle of the road.

The cause of the neurosis, according to Freud, was a real-life challenge in which he had to decide whether to make a wealthy marriage, following his father's wishes, or whether to pursue his own life and marry the lady he loved despite her poverty. The neurosis led to an incapacity for work, which postponed both his education and the decision.

The patient's ambivalent feelings about his father, who reportedly sometimes had a passionate, violent, and often uncontrolled temper, emerge repeatedly in the material. Even at age 27 (several years after his father's death), while having sexual intercourse he thought, "This is glorious—one might murder one's father for this!"—an echo from the childhood neurosis. At 21, after his father died, he developed a compulsion to masturbate. Later, in a complex ritual, he opened the door for his father in the middle of the night; then, coming back into the hall, he took out his penis and looked at it in the mirror. This act seemed to be related to a memory he reported of his father's beating him for masturbation; during this beating, his father had apparently been overcome by what Freud called "elemental fury." Although it was not repeated, the beating apparently made an important impression on the patient; from that time on the patient described himself as a coward, out of fear of his own potential for rageful violence. (According to the patient's mother, the beating was given between the ages of 3 and 4 and was administered because the patient had bitten someone, rather than as punishment for masturbation.)

Freud presents a careful solution to the complex story of the rat torture and the need to repay the money to prevent the torture from being inflicted upon his father or the lady he had admired; the solution is based on symbolic interpretations of the meaning of the word *rats*. This explanation led to an apparent disappearance of what Freud calls "the patient's rat delirium."

According to Freud, the rat punishment stirred up the patient's anal erotism. Rats are interpreted as representing money, syphilis, the penis, and worms. A rat burrowing into the anus unconsciously became equated with the penis burrowing into the anus. Rats came to represent children who bite people in a rage; when the captain told the rat story, the patient unconsciously felt the desire to bite his cruel father, masked by a more or less conscious, derisive feeling that the same torture should be applied to the captain. A day and a half later, when the captain (unconsciously, the father) asked him to run an errand repaying some money, he thought in a hostile way that he would repay the money when his father and the lady he admired could have children (the patient's admired lady was unable to conceive). This in turn was based on two infantile sexual theories: that men can have children and that babies come from the anus. The lady he admired was condemned to childlessness because her ovaries had been removed; the patient, who was extraordinarily fond of children, hesitated to marry her for this reason.

FREUD'S THEORETICAL APPROACH

The second part of the case history is theoretical and discusses various aspects of the psychodynamics of the obsessive-compulsive neuroses. These aspects involve (1) magical thinking and personal superstitions; (2) the omnipotence of thought (a relic of the megalomania of infancy); (3) obsessive ideas (long-standing formations representing distortions, uncertainty, and doubt) that draw the patient away from reality to abstract subjects; (4) ambivalence, with much repressed sadism; (5) displacement of affect and of ideas; (6) isolation—temporal and spatial—of the idea from the affect and from the world to the isolated life of abstractions; and (7) regression, wherein preparatory acts become the substitute for final decisions and thinking replaces acting. Thus, an obsessive thought, according to Freud, is one whose function is to represent an act regressively.

In the obsessional neuroses, the complex is often retained in the consciousness but with a dissociation of its affect. The starting point of a neurosis may be mentioned in a tone of complete indifference by the patient who is unaware of the significance of the material. The two cardinal symptoms of obsessional neuroses are a tendency to doubt and a recurring sense of compulsion. Fundamentally, a deep ambivalence dominates the patient's life; significant people are both intensely loved and intensely hated. In the obsessional neuroses these emotional attitudes are sharply separated. Freud saw the doubting as a result of this ambivalence, and the sense of compulsion as an attempt to overcompensate for the doubt and uncertainty. Freud applied his description of the omnipotence of the obsessional patient's thoughts—the patient's terror that wishes will come true in the real world and belief in the magical power either to prevent or to make thoughts come true—to understanding various primitive rituals of magic and, of course, religious practices. Just as he believed infantile sexuality to be the root of hysteria, Freud stressed infantile sexuality as leading to a nuclear complex in the obsessional neuroses. As in the case of hysteria, he believed that the unraveling of these nuclear complexes would automatically lead to a resolution of the neuroses.

Muslin (1979) warns us that Freud's understanding and use of transference in this case is still a distance from his more definitive statements about transference in his papers on technique and in his *Introductory Lectures on Psycho-Analysis* (Freud 1917). At this point, transference is no longer thought of as an obstruction to the work of analysis, as Freud (1905) described it in the case of Dora, nor has it yet been conceived of, as Freud would do in 1917, as constituting the "central battlefield" of the analysis. In 1909, Freud was still postulating the main curative factor in psychoanalysis to be the unraveling of the mystery of the patient's symptoms through the recovery of memories, not through the development and interpretation of a transference neurosis.

Muslin (1979) points out:

> Although there have been vignettes of Freud's clinical work subsequent to 1909, reported by him and others, there is no systematic study of his therapeutic activity after that date. It is thus impossible to demonstrate "changes" in his clinical work after 1909; one can only compare and contrast his theoretical statements about transference without being able to compare his clinical performances. [p. 563]

So the argument as to whether Freud actually changed his technique after the case of Paul Lorenz remains unresolved, since we have very little in the way of Freud's own published material on which to make a judgment. Before addressing this question of whether or not Freud is presenting his mature psychoanalytic technique, let us turn to Freud's case report itself.

DETAILS OF THE FIRST TWO SESSIONS

The reader must keep in mind that Freud in this case was attempting to use the transference primarily toward the patient's recovery of repressed memories. In this model, transference interpretations focusing on the analyst are not important, since transference is viewed merely as the vehicle by which memories are uncovered.

Freud mentions that his report is based on notes made on the evening of the day of treatment and is as close as possible to a verbatim report as he could provide. In a footnote (p. 159), he again warns us (see Chapter 1) against the practice of taking notes during the actual session because of the consequent withdrawal of the physician's attention—a withdrawal which Freud feels "does the patient more harm than can be made up for by any increase in accuracy that may be achieved in the reproduction of his case history."

> Freud begins by reporting that the patient impressed him as clear-headed and shrewd. Since the patient introduced himself in the initial face-to-face session with a description of his sexual life, Freud reasonably asked what it was that made him lay such stress on this aspect of his history. The patient replied that he learned to do this out of what he knew about Freud's theories. Freud tells us that the patient had actually read none of his writings except for "turning over the pages" of his *The Psychopathology of Everyday Life* (1901). In this book the patient noted an explanation of some verbal associations which reminded him of some of his own "efforts of thought"; this, said the patient, made him decide to put himself in Freud's hands.

To say the least, this constitutes a curious opening. One might suspect that the patient was starting off by flattering Freud, since he claimed to know about Freud's theories although he had not actually read any of Freud's work. In a sense he began by trying to get in "through the back door" by using flattery to gain Freud's acceptance.

There are several ways to listen to this material. Using the traditional psychoanalytic drive/conflict/defense model, one could conceive of it in terms of a disguised anal intrusion of some sort, either involving homosexual urges ("he decided to put himself in my hands" [p. 159]) or anal sadistic urges, or both, which would certainly be consistent with the patient's case history as it later unfolds.

From the object relations model, one might characterize the attempt at flattery as the patient's defense against his immediate sadistic transference feelings toward the authority figure, who, by projective identification, he conceives of as cruel and dangerous. He hopes to lead the therapist astray by hiding these feelings and at the same time to achieve sadistic gratification and revenge by blocking the therapist's efforts to actually understand him. Interesting evidence for this is presented in the original record of the case, where the patient erroneously assumes that a murderer, Leopold Freud, is Freud's relative. Freud writes, "He thought that if there were murderous impulses in my family, I should fall on him like a beast of prey to search out what was evil in him" (p. 285). The patient, who, as we have seen, began by flattering Freud, admits that he actually began the analysis with great mistrust because of this.

From the self-psychology model, this initial flattery and compliance could represent the beginning of an idealizing transference. In my experience with patients who have begun therapy by mentioning that they have read my publications, it is not uncommon for them to have formed an idealization and a highly imaginative fantasy about my alleged "fame," an imagined greatness with which the patient wishes to merge and to share with me. Kohut (1971, 1977) described how uncomfortable such idealization can make the therapist.

The phenomenological model shows that something is inauthentic because the patient is beginning the therapy with a lie, stating that he knows of Freud's theories but actually having read almost nothing about them. The interactive model draws our attention to the therapist's asking, *in the very beginning of the treatment*, "What made you lay such stress upon telling me about your sexual life?" It would not be surprising on the basis of such a question that the transference will be further shaped in some sort of sexual direction.

Lipton (1977a) correctly points out that the first paragraph of Freud's report of his brief introductory face-to-face interview with Paul Lorenz would not be considered sufficient today as a proper diagnostic evaluation. Freud depended on a trial of analysis rather than on diagnostic interviews, and

Lipton defends this technique, although most authors today prefer to do a careful initial face-to-face diagnostic evaluation. The dangers of doing only a brief diagnostic evaluation and proceeding immediately to a trial analysis today include some potential legal problems.

> The language of the first analytic session is striking: "The next day I made him pledge himself to submit . . ." (p. 159). This is Freud's way of introducing free association to the patient, getting the patient to say everything that came into his head. Apparently the patient pledged himself to submit, because Freud says, "I then gave him leave" to begin with any subject he pleased.

It is clear from the beginning that the therapist is taking an authoritative, actively participatory stance in this treatment.

> The patient began by telling Freud of two friends whom he idealized and whom he used for moral support, to raise his self-esteem. He confessed to these friends about his criminal impulses. The first of these two friends betrayed him: It seemed that this individual was really interested in the patient's sister and had used the friendship in order to gain admission to the patient's house. The patient described this as "the first great blow of his life" (p. 160). He then launched without transition into a long confessional about his infantile sexual experiences, including a mention that, at the age of 6, he had "suffered from erections" and had complained about this to his mother. He continued by describing his feeling that there was a connection between this and his inquisitiveness. Already at that age he had the morbid idea that his parents knew his thoughts and that something terrible would happen if he had a wish to see girls naked. Freud's reported intervention at this point was a question about these fears, to which the patient answered, "for instance, that my father might die." The report of the

> session concludes with Freud's dramatic comment about the patient's current obsessional fears regarding the death of his father, which were already reported in the patient's opening statement at the beginning of treatment. The astonishing fact is that the patient's father had already died several years previously.

Freud next breaks off the case narrative and proceeds into a dynamic formulation of the patient's symptoms, which present all the aspects of a challenging intellectual game. Obsessive-compulsive neurotics often disclose their symptoms in a teasing manner, a little bit at a time, and they are very good at the intellectual game of offering and interpreting symbols. The danger with such patients is that the therapist will fall into this game instead of concentrating on eliciting from the patient an answer to the critical question, "How do you feel about that?"

In the traditional drive/conflict/defense view, we might see the patient as again teasing Freud in an anal sadistic fashion by presenting this enticing but paradoxical story. The interactive model would emphasize how the therapist has perhaps invited this kind of transference interaction by his authoritative stance and his obvious great interest in the intellectual unraveling of the mystery of the symptoms. The self-psychological stance might stress the patient's need for reassurance and acceptance from the therapist, coming to treatment much as he had gone to his two friends, and perhaps earlier to his mother, in search of some self/selfobject relationship in order to boost his self-esteem. The phenomenological view would focus on the strangeness of the developing relationship between the patient and Freud that is already apparent in this first analytic session, an encounter in which the patient is "confessing" and Freud is "astonished" and clearly intellectually fascinated. Object relations theorists would emphasize, as Freud does in his discussion, that at the age of 6 or 7, this patient already suffered from a full-blown-neurosis involving, of course, his parents, and they would watch for the projection of various self and object representations onto the therapist in order to more fully understand this childhood neurosis.

> The second session was very dramatic. The patient began with a description of the experience that had caused him to seek treatment, but after he described a cruel military captain who told him about a horrible torture, Lorenz broke off his narrative and "got up from the sofa and begged me to spare him the recital of the details." Freud tactfully insisted on the details and even encouraged the patient by adding "into his anus" to the description, while assuring the patient that he had no taste for cruelty and no desire to torment him. He noted a strange facial expression, which seemed to be related to the patient's wish that this should happen to the lady he admired, although the patient claimed that such thoughts were foreign and repugnant to him.
>
> Lorenz continued by again startling Freud, because it turned out that another idea had occurred to the patient, of this punishment being applied to his father—a completely nonsensical fear since his father was dead. The patient proceeded with a long, complicated story full of self-contradictions and hopeless confusion. Freud got him to tell the story at least three times, and by the end of this second session "the patient behaved as though he were dazed and bewildered. He repeatedly addressed me as 'Captain,' probably because at the beginning of the hour I had told him that I myself was not fond of cruelty like Captain N., and that I had no intention of tormenting him unnecessarily" (p. 169).

The patient has clearly, to some extent in response to Freud's approach, developed an intense and almost immediate transference reaction in which he insists that, regardless of Freud's disclaimers, Freud is cruel and sadistic like the captain. An interactive stance might lead one to ask if Freud at this point was not actually being cruel and sadistic as well as kind to this patient, in parallel to the patient's reportedly sometimes kind and gentle and sometimes hot-tempered father. One might view this as Freud's promoting acting out in the transference rather than interpreting it. There was enough kindness in Freud so that he could be placed in the position of the patient's authoritative father, but the patient also, if we interpret from the interactive point of view, apparently needed a cruel and sadistic captain with whom to collide without destruction, in the nature of a corrective emotional experience. The value of this stance shows itself here because it leads us to focus next on Freud's actual participation in his psychoanalytic cases.

FREUD'S ANALYTIC STANCE

Although Freud showed an intense desire to understand the patient and certainly did not display any fits of temper toward him—he was in some ways extremely benign to him—Freud's personality carried enough forcefulness (or countertransference) to bear a resemblance to both sides of the patient's father—the kind, gentle side and the harsh, hot-tempered side—so that the patient could fasten upon Freud's personality and receive a corrective emotional experience, even though this was not Freud's manifest intent. This case has led some therapists astray in that Freud's exposition emphasizes symbolic and intellectual material; in my opinion, however, the key to the success of the treatment is Freud's personality as well as his focus on the patient's *feelings* in the transference. One cannot help but wonder if such a case—in which during the second session the dazed and bewildered patient calls the analyst "captain" and arises from the sofa—would these days be considered a suitable case for formal psychoanalysis.

Perhaps the best place to mark the development of the transference is in the discussion of the fee, mentioned later in the presentation. Freud, in his characteristically keen way, observed that the florin notes with which the patient paid his fees were invariably clean and smooth. Later, Freud discovered that when he had told the patient his hourly fee, Lorenz had thought to himself, "So many florins, so many rats" (p. 213) and had related this thought to a whole complex of money interests that centered around his father's legacy to him. The cruel captain's request that the patient repay charges due upon a packet connects father, son, captain, money, rats, and Freud. Later, in an important transference dream, the patient dreamed that he saw Freud's daughter with two patches of dung in place of eyes; it is not difficult to see this as a punishment for Freud's taking money from the patient.

Returning to the second dramatic session in which the patient insisted that Freud was the captain, Lorenz, as we have seen, broke off when describing the rat torture and got up from the sofa, begging Freud to spare him the recital of the details. Freud was gentle but relentless at this point and even tried to say some of the repulsive phrases for the patient; he does not mention whether or not he ordered the patient back onto the sofa, but he probably did not, since we are told later (p. 209) that at other times the patient would get up from the sofa and roam around the room.

Lorenz seems to have experienced the second session as some sort of a beating or torment; the patient appears to have set up this situation out of an intense need to act out in the rapidly formed transference. Clearly, whether Freud liked it or not, the patient was unconsciously determined to experience him as he had experienced his father. As Freud later wrote, "Things soon reached a point at which, in his dreams, his waking phantasies, and his associations, he began heaping the grossest and filthiest abuse upon me and my family, though in his deliberate actions he never treated me with anything but the greatest respect" (p. 209). This behavior labels the treatment truly psychoanalytic (whether or not one wishes to call it a formal psychoanalysis), and indicates good potential for uncovering in the transference, regardless of the "irregularities" or parameters introduced by either party.

The patient eventually explained that in roaming around the room he was avoiding physical nearness to Freud for fear of receiving a beating. Freud wrote dramatically, "If he stayed on the sofa he behaved like some one in desperate terror trying to save himself from castigations of terrific violence; he would bury his head in his hands, cover his face with his arm, jump up suddenly and rush away, his features distorted with pain, and so on" (p. 209).

Freud's general reaction to all this material seems to have been the model of the analyst's analyzing attitude: He remained relatively calm and free of anxiety, while constantly attempting to understand and explain the material. Freud was able to maintain this stance because, although the patient was dramatizing his fears and had many destructive fantasies toward Freud and his family, in his deliberate actions and throughout the course of the excellent therapeutic alliance, he was consistently proper and polite, never attempting to act out any of his fantasies toward Freud or others. (Remember that the patient had characterized himself as basically a coward.) It was the patient' ability to maintain the separation between his appropriate behavior and his irrational raging transference fantasies that permitted him to receive a successful uncovering psychotherapy.

At the same time, there is no question that Freud, as usual, was very forceful in his interpretations and in his authoritative conviction of the accuracy of his explanations and interpretations. Based on the patient's material, Freud engaged in an intellectual, philosophical dialogue or "conversation" (p. 185) with the patient, replete with explanations and arguments; Freud was an active psychotherapist in the intellectual sphere. In this situation again, Freud is certainly taking the position of the captain or the leader, consistent with the authoritative role of the Viennese physician at the turn of the century.

This does *not* constitute a criticism of Freud as a therapist or a person, for his intuitive handling of the patient was brilliant. His basic approach was tolerant, reasonable, and consistent with what one would have expected from a reputable and ethical physician of his time; the patient took advantage of the unavoidably assertive aspects of Freud's personality to reenact for himself a dramatic transference in which he feared an extremely quick-tempered father, and simultaneously to re-experience a relationship with the kindlier aspect of his father.

Whether Lorenz's father actually was sometimes subject to a violent, hot temper or not is beside the point. Even if it represents a projection, Lorenz needed to master his fear of attack by the father figure. When the kindness and understanding of Freud permitted him to do this, and when in the therapy he was able to discharge his rage and hatred of his father onto Freud as a transference figure without suffering the feared retaliation, he settled down into a comforting pupil–teacher interaction and his symptoms abated. The transference was not formally interpreted or resolved, but used rather to effect discharge and revival of memories of father-hatred (Muslin 1979).

In a sense, the patient provided himself with a corrective emotional experience; Freud's brilliance as an intuitive psychotherapist was that he allowed the patient to do this. Freud's gratification in the case seems to have come from unraveling the intricate intellectual mysteries of the patient's obsessional symptomatology. Freud's personality and intellectual curiosity were assertive enough to make a transference resemblance possible; at the same time, he provided instances of extremely kind behavior, which fit the gentle side of the patient's father's nature.

Note, for example, in the original record of the case, that Freud sent his patient a postcard, perhaps from one of his vacation trips. The postcard is signed "cordially" (p. 293), which the patient protests is too intimate. At another point, one of the most dramatically cryptic statements ever written by Freud (although not intended for publication) appears: "Dec. 28.—He was hungry and was fed" (p. 303). These direct acts of kindness toward the patient stirred up the ambivalent response that is characteristic of obsessional patients; they also give a glimpse of Freud's basic and consistently humane attitude toward his patients—he was anything but disinterested and impersonal.

At one point Freud asked the patient to bring a photograph of the lady he admired, an act which precipitated what Freud described as "Violent struggle, bad day" (p. 260).The patient was in conflict about leaving the treatment at this point. Still, depending on one's theoretical approach, some therapists feel that it is an acceptable technical procedure during uncovering psychotherapy to ask certain carefully selected patients to bring photographs of the significant people in their lives, because a photograph helps to fix in the therapist's mind the person being talked about and brings home to the patient the intensity and the seriousness of the psychoanalytic inquiry (as well as providing a mirroring experience if the therapist responds appropriately to the photograph). This is a deliberate technical procedure, however, and the countertransference and transference ramifications and effects of it must be kept clearly in mind and must be fearlessly explored. Very complicated situations can result. For example, during a previous psychoanalysis, one of my patients had brought in several childhood pictures at the request of the analyst, who then asked to keep them for a few days to look them over. When the patient subsequently wanted them back, the analyst discovered that he had lost them. The patient "forgave" him, but an unanalyzed "negative transference" remained, and the patient subsequently required reanalysis. Was this transference? The answer is not simple, since such incidents can easily serve to mask deeper unconscious distortions coming from the patient.

What do we do with a patient who breaks off in the second session, gets up from the couch, and begs the therapist to spare him the recital of details? Is such a patient analyzable? Should we switch to supportive psychotherapy? Our skillful listening will determine how we respond to what we hear in the patient's request. Freud clearly believed that the patient was analyzable, and he had some awareness that he was being set up to be the cruel captain. He was willing to allow the patient to develop this transference even though it made him uncomfortable and compelled him to issue a disclaimer.

Is it empathic to demand that the patient continue with something from which he begs to be spared? What sort of transference would have developed if Freud had said something like, "No, it is not necessary to recite these details at this time; perhaps at a later date when you are more comfortable." Such a response would have been inconsistent with Freud's starting the therapy by demanding that the patient take a pledge to say everything that comes to his mind. From the beginning of therapy, our listening stance is reflected in how we present the fundamental rule to the patient. Suppose that Freud, instead of demanding a pledge, had requested, "Try to say as much as you can that occurs to you" or "Do your best to say whatever comes to your mind." Freud's relentless and dedicated pursuit of the truth in his practice of psychoanalysis was used by the patient to set Freud up in the transference as a cruel and sadistic captain.

The very serious danger of a potential transference psychosis emerges in this session. A patient who actually begins to address the therapist as "Captain" and who seems dazed in the second session should be watched very carefully for further manifestations of transference psychosis. This patient was apparently able at the end of each session to pull himself sharply back together and to maintain a normal professional relationship with Freud; that is, the regression existed only during the sessions. This is an important signal to watch for, as one would not wish to send a patient out of the office who is wandering around in a dazed fashion and addressing the therapist as "Captain."

The patient tormented Freud by reciting his long, paradoxical, complicated history, and by the end of the second session Freud was deeply immersed in the intellectual game of trying to make sense of it and to recognize symbols, displacements, and memories. It is clear that his therapeutic stance in this case at this time revolved around the notion that psychoanalytic cure is a function of the clarification and recovery of repressed memories and infantile conflicts as they appear disguised in symptoms and in the transference. Phenomenologically, the patient clearly insisted on reliving and acting out a crucial conflict in the relationship with Freud, and if this is true, then the complicated case material he presented should be considered a part of the acting out, rather than requiring interpretation of details and symbols as a fundamental part of the curative process. From this point of view both the patient's behavior and mode of narrative represent the patient's way of relating to other people, of his being-in-the-world.

DETAILS OF THE THIRD THROUGH SEVENTH SESSIONS

> During the third session, Lorenz continued his long, complicated, obsessional story while Freud listened quietly. Freud seems to have spent the entire session trying to get the story straight. In startling contrast to the second session, this session is very intellectual and undramatic.

The patient's ability to come into the third session and, rather than continue to dramatically deteriorate, proceed with an intellectual discussion of a complex story clearly displays his defensive capacity, as is typical of obsessive-compulsive neurotics, to use intellectualization to protect against psychotic disintegration. Freud, either knowingly or intuitively, supports this defense by working actively with the patient to clarify the details of this complex narrative. Freud is thus performing a supportive function at this point, typical of his intuitive genius at the art of psychotherapy. Even in the most rigorous and traditional psychoanalysis, there are some periods when the patient needs supportive therapy or when the anxiety becomes so overwhelming that the treatment itself is endangered. This is a good example. Regardless of the listening stance used, Freud's procedure is required at this point, a form of holding while uncovering.

Depending on which channel of attunement is employed, the question that would be debated is, What was the meaning and importance of Lorenz's long and complex story? Freud took it very seriously, as already noted. Self psychologists would stress the supportive or soothing aspect of the therapy, in which both partners work intellectually together, perhaps in an alter-ego selfobject transference (Kohut 1984). From an interactive point of view, this kind of complex obsessional material is stimulated by the therapist's obvious interest in the intellectual game involved. An object relations approach would stress the sadistic, teasing manner in which the story is clarified a little bit at a time. Some sort of anal withholding is involved here such that the therapist is compelled to continuously wait for a little more clarification. A power struggle with the projected sadistic parent is enacted.

> Freud began the fourth session with a question: "And how do you intend to proceed today?"

This apparently kindly question stands in interesting juxtaposition to Freud's more authoritative demand at the beginning of treatment that the patient make a pledge to submit to a fundamental rule. It again shows Freud's combination of authoritative firmness and kind supportiveness, which seems to be the very thing the patient needs in the treatment. An important alternative approach in beginning the ordinary session is for the therapist to remain silent until the patient broaches some topic. If the patient continues to remain silent, the usual procedure after a few moments is to ask the patient what comes to mind. One can only wonder why Freud decided to begin the fourth session with this benign question. A guess might be that he was relieved that the third session did not proceed in the same manner as the second, but that the patient had evidenced the capacity to use intellectual defenses. Regressive disintegration during therapy sessions is draining and exhausting for both patient and therapist, even when it is controlled and confined to the session.

> The patient proceeded to tell "at great length" the story of his father's last illness. He listed his own symptoms involving his father. Freud responded by giving the patient a lecture on the "underlying principles of psycho-analytic therapy" (p. 175)

The interaction at this point has shifted to one of teacher and pupil and continues as a partly supportive psychotherapy. An alternative to this approach might simply be silence on the part of the therapist. Freud often felt called upon to offer lectures and explanations in his therapeutic work, as he considered psychoanalysis a form of after-education (Freud 1940). The countertransference aspects of this are not explored, nor were they probably even recognized in 1909. From a self-psychology standpoint, the patient has already informed Freud of the importance of the alter-ego relationship. His symptoms were incapacitating, and he has reported that only the consolation given by a friend enabled him to go on. Therefore, Freud is clearly responding empathically to the patient's plight.

> The fifth session began with the patient's doubts and arguments about Freud's lecture. Freud responded with more lectures and explanations. The session ends with Freud's mentioning "a word or two upon the good opinion

> I had formed of him, and this gave him visible pleasure" (p. 178).

Freud's supportive stance clearly continued in the fifth session, and now teacher and pupil are together harmoniously, in dramatic contrast to the patient and the sadistic captain couple in the second session. One also gets the impression that Freud is relieved and much prefers the teacher–pupil couple to the patient–captain couple. Freud did not hesitate to actively reassure the patient and to offer him praise. This analytic stance is a far cry from that of the neutral, opaque mirror and the attitude akin to that of the surgeon, which Freud advocates in his papers on technique.

Lipton (1979) casts doubt on Strachey's translation where Freud is said to have added a "word or two upon the good opinion I had formed of him." This "word or two," writes Lipton, did not appear in the German text of the case, and in Freud's original notes it actually seems to have been a compliment on the clarity of the patient's presentation of some characteristics of his symptoms. This conceptualization places Freud's comment in a less seductive context and focuses it on the patient's actual material.

> The sixth session began with another long story from the patient's childhood, in which the patient eventually admitted the notion that his father's death would make him rich enough to marry the lady he admired. Freud continued the teacher–pupil stance by objecting, interrupting, clarifying and explaining. He even launched into a discussion of Shakespeare's *Julius Caesar*, and in a footnote he concedes, "It is never the aim of discussions like this to create conviction" (p. 181). What he wished to do was to bring the material to the patient's attention, facilitate the

> emergence of fresh material from the unconscious, and heighten conflictual areas for the patient's consideration. The intellectual dialectic between the patient and Freud continued to the end of the session, with Freud attempting to set up a reconstruction of the patient's early childhood.

Clearly this session represents an acting out on the part of the therapist. The patient's behavior in relation to the therapist is unrecognized; the transference is neither alluded to nor identified. There is little observation of the patient's behavior from the transference point of view, even while Freud is offering deep genetic interpretations, speculations, explanations, and reconstructions. There is a narcissistic aspect to the therapist that shows itself in this sixth session in the therapist's apparent compulsion to explain, offer literary allusions, and generally treat the patient as a student. The patient eagerly enjoyed this interaction because it is clear that he is the teacher's favored student, and he has already been praised by Freud, so there is a collusion between the couple for a mutually gratifying acting out.

This is an extremely valuable session for the beginning psychotherapist to study because it comprises a form of acting out that very often takes place between an insufficiently analyzed therapist and a clever, interesting, or intellectual patient. Silence as a response to this material might be the best way to allow the transference to develop further. From the self-psychology stance, silence would probably lead to the patient's increasing discomfort as he or she seeks to elicit mirroring from the idealized therapist, and could eventually lead to an interpretation of what the patient is seeking.

From an object relations point of view, this session represents what Langs (1978) refers to as a Type B field, in which the treatment is dominated by derivatives of patient–

therapist interaction rather than by material emerging primarily from the patient's unconscious.

Phenomenologically, the patient has engineered an encounter between himself and this most famous psychoanalyst that is very gratifying for the patient; he is temporarily one of Freud's favored pupils. Over Freud's lifetime, a number of rather disturbed individuals insinuated themselves into this position. In at least one instance, that of Victor Tausk (Roazen 1969), sudden loss of this position of being one of Freud's favored pupils led to a suicide. This evidences a harsh side to Freud. He could in certain instances be very wounding and could abruptly thrust someone who had felt himself or herself in a favored position sharply away from him. Further evidence of such a hostile side is manifested in his response to Horney's challenge to his views on female sexuality (Quinn 1987). When Freud made up his mind that someone was out of the psychoanalytic mainstream, he simply thrust him or her out of sight, and his followers subsequently treated that individual as a nonperson with views not worth considering.

The traditional analytic view would take the material of this session very seriously despite the countertransference acting out because it deals with the death of the patient's father and points to the emergence of the oedipal struggle, a struggle that is never very far from the surface in this patient's stories and transference manifestations.

By the end of the sixth session, the acute listener might begin to wonder about the focus of this case. In the technique of psychoanalytic listening, the best clue to the focus of the material is contained in that part which is most dramatic and affect-laden. Thus far the second session is the most dramatic, and the third, fourth, and fifth sessions represent a retreat away from the patient's quasi-psychotic transference experience in the second session. The focus of the material, therefore, is the patient's attempt to defend, by a variety of symptoms and intellectualizations, against some kind of extremely hostile and frightening interaction with a sadistic parent figure. Whether this parent is the father or the mother cannot really be determined, even though the focus in the second session is on a hostile male parent figure. One can only speculate at this point as to whether this is primarily an oedipal neurosis or a defense against an underlying paranoia, or against preoedipal conflicts involving the patient's mother. Intuitively, Freud has not allowed the transference to become psychotic, as it threatened to do in the second session; rather, he has succeeded in "holding" the patient and supporting his intellectual defenses, at least until such time as the patient becomes more comfortable and can deal with this intense material.

> The seventh session, the last one reported in detail, continued with the same subject: the question of whether the patient had a long-repressed death wish toward his father. The session proceeded in a very intellectual fashion, and this time the patient in his turn made a literary allusion—to a famous saying of Nietzsche from *Beyond Good and Evil*. Freud maintained his supportive role and attempted to alleviate the patient's guilt by providing explanations and lectures. He adds in a footnote, "I only produced these arguments so as once more to demonstrate to myself their inefficacy" (p. 185). He became more instructive as the session reached the end, and at one point, when the patient expressed doubt about whether all his evil impulses came from his infantile predispositions, Freud reports, "I promised to prove it to him in the course of the treatment" (p. 186). Freud ends the seventh session as an authoritative physician, explaining to the patient that a normal period of mourning would last from one to two years, but a pathological one, like the patient's, would last indefinitely.

Freud seems to have had the habit of making promises to patients. For example, he promised the Wolf Man (Freud 1918b) that he would cure his gastrointestinal symptoms. Indeed, Gedo and Goldberg (1973) refer to Freud's promise that the patient's constipation would be cured as evidence that "because this intervention was never resolved through interpretation, the technique of the treatment cannot be viewed as psychoanalytic from today's vantage point" (p. 187). This, of course, represents narcissistic countertransference acting out on the part of the therapist, but one must remember that Freud's boundless confidence that he could unravel the mysterious intricacies of symptoms was an important curative factor for many of his patients.

The basic premise of Freud's traditional psychoanalytic approach was that the irrational could be made rational. Later in the case of Paul Lorenz (p. 209), Freud further describes the vivid excitement of this patient's treatment, which seemed to oscillate between a harmonious teacher–pupil relationship and an intense transference situation in which even the couch itself became charged as a torture table. Although the therapy was very dramatic, Freud conceived of it as efficacious primarily because the patient gained intellectual understanding by means of suffering through a transference repetition of his childhood.

THE ROLE OF TRANSFERENCE AND COUNTERTRANSFERENCE

Zetzel (1966) published a brief paper on "Freud's Rat Man," further investigating the dynamics of the case. She helps to revive for us what happened at the death of the patient's older sister, which took place when he was between 3 and 4 years of age; it was at this time that his father had allegedly given him the beating. The death of his sister at the height of his infantile neurosis set this patient on the path toward becoming a "decompensated obsessional neurotic" instead of a "well-integrated somewhat obsessional character," says Zetzel. She explains that his positive identification with Freud as a father surrogate "may have been the central factor which impelled him towards greater mastery of unresolved intrapsychic conflict" (p. 228).

Gedo and Goldberg (1973) carried this investigation further by reminding us that Zetzel also maintained that the patient was unable to grieve or to accept the finality of his father's death. Zetzel quoted from Freud's notes: "I pointed out to him that this attempt to deny the reality of his father's death is the basis of his whole neurosis" (Freud 1909, p. 300). Gedo and Goldberg explain that this patient demonstrates Freud's concept of disavowal—what Kohut (1971) has called the "vertical split." According to Zetzel, this disavowal occurred in Paul Lorenz because he could not deal with the prior trauma of his sister's death, presumably because he experienced his sexual and hostile impulses as the cause of the tragedy. The disavowal produced "a chronic split in the self as the outcome of unmanageable stress" (Gedo and Goldberg 1973, p. 113) in which one aspect of the self remained at the level of magical thinking and grandiosity—outstanding regressive features in Paul Lorenz's case, as in the case of many obsessional neurotics.

Kanzer (1952) claims that Freud's reply when Lorenz begged Freud to spare him recital of the details of the punishment—that he had no taste whatever for cruelty and no desire to torment him—led Lorenz to equate Freud with the captain. Gill and Muslin (1976) argue to the contrary that Lorenz had already developed this transference and that it persisted *despite* Freud's remark. They maintain that Freud's reply was tantamount to a transference interpretation, saying in effect that the patient was mistakenly identifying him with the cruel captain. This early interpretation of transference was both an explanation and an effort to avoid the potentially treatment-disruptive repercussions of the transference. This depiction is more congruent with Freud's general behavior toward the patient. Gill and Muslin see this case as a demonstration that early interpretation of transference is sometimes necessary in order to avoid the development of an unmanageable transference.

It does not follow from this that the treatment technique used today is *better* than Freud's approach in this case. The so-called modern technique, according to Lipton (1977a), carries a disadvantageous trend. Lipton states that the common assumption is that Freud changed his technique after this case, but he objects to this assumption, noting that Freud was very cordial to his patients and left a positive transference of affection and friendship during and after the treatment. Lipton argues that the meticulous attempt to avoid the "minor" or "trivial" interventions that Freud made in this case—an avoidance now considered crucial by some analysts—represents an exclusion of the analyst's personality, which, like too much analytic silence, leads to a dehumanization of the analytic situation and a reactive iatrogenic narcissism. Lipton claims that Freud's recommendations that the analyst should be a blank screen to the patient are with respect to technique, but that he took the analyst's personal cordiality and ethical behavior for granted. He argues that Freud's technique in the case of Lorenz *was* his definitive technique. It was undertaken in 1907, when Freud was 51 years old, at the peak of his mental powers and with 21 years of experience in private practice.

Momigliano (1987) investigated Freud's technique between 1920 and 1938 by reviewing published testimony of Freud's analysands during that period. Although such testimony is highly unreliable and self-serving, taken *in toto* it serves as evidence that Freud did not change his technique and that Lipton is correct.

Lipton reviews the adverse comments on Freud's technique, which appeared in the literature about this case only 40 years after it was published, and he defends Freud against these complaints, a debate beyond the scope of this book. He notes that Freud made "no disclosures, no self-revelations, and revealed the contents of his own mind only in a formalistic sense" (p. 258). Freud did not engage in any ramblings about himself in actively trying to form a personal and private relationship with Lorenz. He confined himself to interventions related to the subject of Lorenz's material. This would be a reply to the suggestions previously presented in this chapter that silence might be an alternative response to Lorenz's material; Lipton does not believe that silence would necessarily be "correct" or that talking would be "questionable."

Lipton's point, which should be carefully considered, is that the technique and practice of careful psychoanalytic listening does not imply that one should not be cordial, pleasant, and courteous to one's patients. Indeed it is unempathic to behave in any other fashion, regardless of one's theoretical orientation.

Lipton (1977b) views Freud's activity with Lorenz as based on what Freud (1909, p. 185) called "our conversation" in characterizing his analysis of this patient. Lipton believes that analysis may indeed be described as "conversation," and he reminds us of Freud's (1904) earlier comment, "The session proceeds like a conversation between two people equally awake" (p. 250); one is not required to wait in silence for the analysis to unfold. We should not lose sight of Lipton's (1983) main contention that silent listening is "an *active*, *potent* intervention" (p. 45). In this Lipton distinguishes between the silence that naturally accompanies psychoanalytic listening and silence as a deliberate lack of response to material. For example, in exigencies, as Lipton (1977a) points out, to make no response is an active intervention, and the patient's next material will be a response to that silence.

Thus a countertransference danger exists implicit both in the silence that is inherent in the process of psychoanalytic listening and in the silence that is maintained as a deliberate lack of response to the patient's material. In both cases the silence can be rationalized but is sometimes experienced by the patient as a narcissistic wound. Here everything depends on the skill and personal psychoanalysis of the therapist. For if such a wound *was* intended out of unconscious sadistic countertransference, then the consequences will be disruptive to the treatment. If, on the other hand, it was experienced as wounding out of aspects of the transference, then it should be amenable to interpretation and understanding. Tactful handling of this problem is essential, for, as Lipton (1977a) states:

> The patient often misconstrues the analyst's listening as silence and often attributes important meaning to it. . . . It usually takes some time for the patient to gain confidence that the analyst is indeed listening and is not silent, and the distinction is important. [p. 265]

SIX

LISTENING TO THE NARCISSISTIC PATIENT

IN HIS BOOK *The Art of the Novel*, Milan Kundera (1986) points out how much courage it required to adopt the view of the world developed by Cervantes. Kundera explains:

> As God slowly departed from the seat whence he had directed the universe and its order of values, distinguished good from evil, and endowed each thing with meaning, Don Quixote set forth from his house into a world he could no longer recognize. In the absence of the Supreme Judge, the world suddenly appeared in its fearsome ambiguity; the single divine Truth decomposed into myriad relative truths parceled out by men. [p. 6]

A view that the world is ambiguous, that one is obliged to face, not a single absolute truth, but a welter of contradictory truths, was the point of view of one of the first great novelists.

In Cervantes's work, truths were embodied in imaginary selves called *characters.* Kundera maintains that the only certainty one has in the world of Cervantes is "the wisdom of uncertainty"; to cling to this as the only certainty requires great courage. For Kundera, the novel is a poetic meditation on the enigma of existence and an investigation of human life in the trap that the world has become. In the novel, no one possesses the Truth. Kundera sees this as an antidote to the age of science, an age in which the more humans advance in knowledge, the less clearly they can see either the world as a whole or their own selves. He points out that "Once elevated by Descartes to 'master and proprietor of nature,' man has now become a mere thing to the forces (of technology, of politics, of history) that bypass him, surpass him, possess him" (p. 4).

THE CONTROVERSIAL PSYCHOLOGY OF THE SELF

It was in order to deal with humans in this current post-modern situation, the culture of narcissism (Lasch 1978), that Kohut developed his psychology of the self. Elsewhere I have reviewed Kohut's work in detail and discussed the psychoanalytic treatment of narcissism (Chessick 1985a). The psychology of the self remains even now a highly controversial psychoanalytic theory. Central to this controversy is the issue of whether or not interpretations based on the psychology of the self tend to divert us from and cover over sexual and oedipal material, and lead patients away from facing their nuclear oedipal conflicts. I have already presented an example of this problem in Basch's case of Miss Banks (see Chapter 4).

As a general rule of thumb, one can say that a successful uncovering psychotherapy must contain sharp manifestations of both positive and negative transference. In other words, if one wishes to do psychotherapy, one must be prepared to be exposed to powerful negative and positive emotional feelings from the patient, often on a highly irrational basis. This exposure to such powerful feelings can lead to many mistakes, retreats, and confusions in psychotherapy if therapists are not expecting the feelings, are not prepared to deal with them, or are so primarily preoccupied with their own needs and problems that they cannot clearly perceive what is going on. There is a strong and all-too-human tendency in psychotherapy to deflect emerging manifestations of powerful erotic or negative transferences by various forms of interventions, such as making a joke, lavishing extra kindness on the patient, and so forth, resulting in a collusion (Langs 1982) to avoid these uncomfortable emotions. It is the responsibility of the therapist to prevent this.

Meyers (1981) reports on a panel in which he quotes Kohut as follows:

> In the clinical situation for example, as we listen to our patients' free associations, we will hold both viewpoints in suspension—the classical one that alerts us to the presence of evidence for the transference reactivation of structural conflict, the self-psychological one that alerts us to the presence of evidence for the transference reactivation of thwarted developmental needs—in order to determine which one of them will lead us to the more psychologically valid understanding of the patient. [p. 155]

Kohut is convinced that the psychopathology of many narcissistic patients is more deeply understood and accurately interpreted when viewed within the framework of the psychology of the self, and heard as involving the reactivation of thwarted developmental needs, in contrast to listening and understanding based on the framework of drives and the reactivation of unresolved structural conflict. Kohut admits that this must be further investigated empirically, but he does not suggest what sort of empirical investigation would really persuade him to give up his psychology-of-the-self listening stance.

Kohut also argued at this panel that he did not feel this was the appropriate time to develop a synthesis between the psychology of the self and other schools of psychoanalytic thought. As we shall see in a discussion of his case presentation, the basic difference is that self psychology considers psychological contents as primary that have formerly been considered as secondary and defensive. Furthermore, he claims:

> The self psychologist's understanding of the legitimacy of the needs of the self leads, via a subtle change in the mode of his communications, perhaps in particular via a changed tone of voice, to an atmosphere which is especially in tune with the requirements of the narcissistically damaged patient, as he remobilizes the old childhood needs of a self that strives to achieve vitality, harmony, and coherence. [pp. 157–158]

Ornstein (1981) added to this more generally:

> All too often, and perhaps for long periods, many of us remain within the same mode of listening and attribute lack of progress to the severity of the patient's psychopathology. It is perhaps only in response to stalemates, dropouts, and the return of our patients for a second analysis, that we reflect upon the supposedly unanalyzable nature of the patient's psychopathology and are better able to focus directly on our own analytic approach and the theories that inform our clinical work. [p. 365]

The crucial issue of Kohut's (1979) presentation of the case of Mr. Z., contained in one of his most important papers, is to raise the question of whether a new theory was needed to allow the shift in the analyst's mode of listening that was necessary for the successful analysis of Mr. Z. We know that all vantage points for psychoanalytic listening are ultimately influenced by the particular theories that guide them. In this sense, Ornstein points out, a theory is an observational tool, although it is ultimately the accumulation of empirical clinical data, not our theories, that provides the most secure base for our knowledge.

Critics have argued that the extensive case history of Mr. Z. provided insufficient evidence for Kohut's self-psychology hypotheses, since the case material could be interpreted in a variety of ways. For example, Edelson (1984) claimed that Kohut showed no understanding of "what is required to make convincing the argument that evidence he presents is related probatively to his hypothesis" (p. 61). To answer his critics, Kohut (1984) wrote:

> Case histories – not to speak of the brief case vignettes that I often use in my writings – can never be more than illustrative; they are a special means of communication within the professional community intended to clarify scientific information from a clinical researcher to his colleagues. [p. 89]

THE CASE OF MR. Z.: THE FIRST ANALYSIS

Mr. Z. was a graduate student in his mid-20s when he first consulted Kohut.

> Kohut described Mr. Z. as handsome and muscular, with a pale, sensitive face, "the face of a dreamer and thinker." He

> lived with his widowed mother in comfortable financial circumstances because his father, a successful business executive, had died four years earlier, leaving a considerable fortune. Mr. Z. was an only child. His vague complaints involved mild somatic symptoms such as extrasystoles, sweaty palms, abdominal fullness, and either constipation or diarrhea. He felt socially isolated and was unable to form relationships with girls; his grades were good, but he felt that he was functioning below his capacities. He was lonely and had only one friend, unmarried, who also had trouble in his relationships with women. A few months before the patient consulted Kohut, this friend became attached to a woman and lost interest in seeing Mr. Z.

Kohut (1979) describes this as a "defensively established threesome" (p. 4) involving Mr. Z., his friend, and Mr. Z.'s mother. Kohut believed that the dropping out of Mr. Z.'s friend was the event that probably precipitated his seeking analysis, and that his vague complaints and mild somatic symptoms, having developed during the few months prior to seeing Kohut, were probably triggered by the precipitating event. The deeper problems, such as the patient's social isolation, difficulty in establishing relationships with women, loneliness, and academic functioning below his capacities, were of much longer duration and were indicative of character pathology. An attempt to outline the essential dynamics of his character pathology at this point, regardless of the listening stance used, would be sheer speculation. Ornstein (1981) agrees with this contention.

> Masturbatory fantasies, in which the patient submissively performed menial tasks in the service of a domineering woman, were always sadomasochistic. Yet he insisted that as far back as he could remember, he had an excellent

> relationship with his mother. When he was $3\frac{1}{2}$ years old, Mr. Z.'s father became seriously ill and was hospitalized for several months; during this time his father fell in love with a nurse who had taken care of him. He did not return home but went instead to live with the nurse for about a year and a half, rarely visiting the family. There was no divorce, and when the patient was 5 years old, his father returned home.
>
> In the masturbation fantasies, the woman was imagined as "being strong, demanding, and insatiable" (p. 4). The patient compared his experience at the moment of ejaculation to that of a horse made to pull a load too heavy for its powers and driven by the coachman's whip to give its last ounce of strength, "or similar to Roman galley slaves whipped on by their overseer during a sea battle" (p. 4).

Our five listening stances would offer five different interpretations of this patient's masturbatory fantasies. Freud's drive/conflict/defense orientation would stress the oedipal aspect of the fantasies, perhaps based on a sadomasochistic conception of the primal scene. The object relations listening stance would focus on the intrapsychic representation of the mother as strong, demanding, and insatiable, and the patient's self-representation as that of a slave who is not up to the tasks placed upon him. A listener using the phenomenological approach would associate immediately to Hegel's (1807) famous description of the master and the slave in *Phenomenology of Spirit* (Section 4). Here the emphasis is on the great need that each individual in this sadomasochistic dyad has for the other in order to mutually define their self-representations. The patient's productivity defines him as an individual, whereas the domineering woman is actually dependent for her self-definition as master on the patient's productivity in this situation, so that the patient's self is actually better defined than that of the woman. This is consistent with Hegel's ingenious description of the dialectical determination of self-consciousness, and gives us an indication of the level of integration of both the patient and his mother.

The interactive approach would stress Kohut's comment that the details of Mr. Z.'s problems were revealed "at first very slowly and against resistance motivated by shame" (p. 4). The interactive therapist might even wonder whether the patient's report of sadomasochistic masturbation fantasies at this point in the therapy indicated the presence of an already-developed transference, one in which the patient experienced the therapist as the domineering, insatiable, and strong woman who was drawing out of him the work that he in turn was desperately straining to offer in accordance with the therapist's demands.

> The patient's mother had been quite young when he was born, and he had an intense relationship with her. According to the patient, "he was the apple of her eye" (p. 4). The father was also pleased with him as far as could be judged. After the father returned home following his escapade with the nurse, the marriage remained unhappy, as one might expect.
>
> Kohut reported that in the transference during the first year of the treatment, the patient demanded exclusive control and admiration, as if from a doting mother. Kohut confronted the patient many times with the reconstruction that during the oedipal period his mother, especially in the absence of siblings and of his father, devoted her total attention to the patient.

Thus Kohut is interpreting the transference as a narcissistic situation hiding the wish for an oedipal victory, "a regressive mother transference" (p. 5). This is completely in accord with the standard drive/conflict/defense orientation, in which oedipal wishes are treated as central and the narcissistic aspects of the patient are thought to represent a defensive maneuver designed to hide the basic wish to possess the mother sexually, and perhaps to gain delusory compensation for the lack of gratification of this oedipal drive.

The phenomenological listening stance would point out the similarity in the struggle between the master and the slave in the patient's masturbation fantasies and between the patient and the analyst in the initial transference situation. Focus might be on the centrality of the patient's effort to define himself and his ego boundaries by means of this struggle in order to gain a sense of worthiness and autonomy. This attempt to form identity through opposition, rather than self-actualization through the free choice of one's own project, represents an inauthentic life-style, an "escape from freedom" (Fromm 1941). The interactive point of view might remind us that the power struggle reflected in this transference is another version of the difficulty Mr. Z. had in revealing his weakness—very slowly and shamefully—and his effort to reverse the situation into one in which he could force the analyst to do his bidding.

Thus only the drive/conflict/defense model moves substantially away from the clinical data here and leads us to the more experience-distant hypothesis that the core of this problem is an oedipal fixation; following either the phenomenological, interactive, or—as we will see—the self-psychological approach, we would find ourselves on quite a different path toward understanding this patient.

The object relations approach might be dormant until the following interchange occurred:

> Kohut reported that for a long time, the patient intensely opposed his reconstructions or interpretations. "He blew up in rages against me, time after time—indeed the picture he presented during the first year and a half of the analysis was dominated by his rage" (p. 5). These explosive attacks were evoked either "in response to my interpretations concerning his narcissistic demands and his arrogant feelings of 'entitlement' " (p. 5), or because of various unavoidable interruptions of the treatment due to schedule irregularities or to Kohut's vacations.

The object relations listening view would come into activation here, emphasizing a splitting in which all-bad self and object representations are projected onto the analyst, as a response either to interpretations or to interruptions, which are then used as the triggers that "prove" to the patient that he is being offended by the "all-bad" therapist (Kernberg 1975). It is noteworthy that Kohut offered no interpretation of the projection of split-off all-bad self and object representations to the patient, although the patient repeatedly claimed that his anger was justified because the therapist obstinately failed to admire and obey him. This is true even though the patient reacted to separations with depression, hypochondriasis, and fleeting suicidal thoughts.

What is the source of the patient's explosions in response to Kohut's oedipal interpretations? From a drive/conflict/defense point of view, they reflect the patient's secondary narcissism (Freud 1914b) since he allegedly feels "entitled" to the doting mother. He regresses and clings to his preoedipal narcissistic demands in order to avoid facing the frustrated yearning of a little boy for the sexual possession of his mother. That is, the reactive, or secondary, narcissistic deluded grandiosity represents a regressive denial of the little boy's failure to attain sexual possession of the mother and a compensation for losing her in competition with the father.

The phenomenological point of view would stress the importance of the patient's expression of rage during the first year and a half of his analysis—a situation, it should be noted, in which there was no retaliation or destruction. The picture of the calm, skilled craftsman analyst serving the function of allowing the patient to discover that no harm comes from his verbal expression of rage would represent the treatment process itself at this point. The interactive stance would go further, attempting to focus on the analyst's contribution to the production of this rage, centering on Kohut's phrase "a reconstruction with which I confronted the patient many times" (p. 5). This process of repeatedly confronting a patient with an interpretation or reconstruction often evokes the patient's rage. From an interactive point of view, it represents another facet of a power struggle and a battle for control—in this case mind control—of the patient.

Ostow (1979) claimed that in the first analysis, Kohut missed the contrast between the idyllic relationship that the patient claimed to have had with his mother and the hostility exhibited in the transference. According to Ostow, the transference suggests repressed hostility to the mother, an interpretation that is confirmed by the sadomasochistic masturbation fantasy of enslavement to a woman. This deeply repressed hostility was so strong, and generated so much anxiety and resistance, that it indicated the dominant need was to maintain the attachment to the mother at all costs.

> After about a year and a half, the patient "rather abruptly became much calmer" (p. 5) and stopped complaining that he was not understood. Kohut "remarked approvingly on

> the change" and informed the patient that "the working through of his own narcissistic delusions was now bearing fruit" (p. 5). The patient rejected this explanation but with much less rage than before. The patient claimed that he was less angry because at one point in interpreting his narcissistic demands Kohut had remarked, "Of course it hurts when one is not given what one assumes to be one's due" (p. 5). Kohut regarded this claim as an effort on the patient's part to save face by pinning the change on a relatively insignificant comment with which Kohut had introduced an interpretation. He even considered interpreting this "excuse" as a last-ditch resistance against the patient's fully accepting his grandiosity and narcissism, but he did not do so.

Kohut here interprets the narcissism as protection against the painful awareness of the returned father, a powerful rival who possessed the mother sexually, and against a castration anxiety to which an awareness of his competitive and hostile impulses toward his father would have exposed him. Thus, for Kohut at this point, the axis of the case was a regression to a pregenital drive aim out of fear of taking a competitive stance against the father. The masochism was explained as a sexualization of his guilt about the preoedipal possession of his mother, and about his unconscious oedipal rivalry, using fairly standard traditional drive/conflict/ defense interpretations.

> The patient revealed that at the age of 11 he had been involved in a homosexual relationship with a 30-year-old teacher, the assistant director of his summer camp. The relationship, which consisted mostly of mutual caressing, lasted about two years. The relationship was a happy one for Mr. Z., who idealized his friend. It was destroyed by the

> appearance of pubertal changes in Mr. Z., at which time gross sexuality entered into the picture. Puberty only served to increase Mr. Z.'s sense of social isolation and to tie him more firmly to his mother; there were no heterosexual experiences.
>
> As far back as Mr. Z. could remember, the content of his childhood masturbation fantasies had always been masochistic, and masturbatory activity had begun at about the time of his father's return. The various pregenital material in the reported masturbation fantasies was interpreted by Kohut as based on clinging to pregenital drive aims out of the fear of taking a competitive stance against the father. The patient's sexual life, from the time that he terminated the quasi-homosexual relationship to the time of the analysis, was restricted to an addictive sort of masturbation, with no heterosexual activity.

The object relations point of view would stress the splitting of representations in this case material into the maternal figure, who is experienced in the masturbation fantasies as dominating and unreasonably demanding, on the one hand, and the paternal quasi-homosexual figure, who is experienced as caressing, soothing, and erotically exciting, on the other. It was only when the caressing, soothing interaction with the male camp director became more overtly sexual that the patient had to give it up and retreat into an isolated, asexual life. From the phenomenological point of view, the patient cannot tolerate a frankly heterosexual relationship with a woman, so he chooses either a relationship with a male that is characterized by relatively little overt sexual content, isolated masturbation with sadomasochistic fantasies, or a "closeness" to his mother.

The interactive point of view would emphasize above all

the dramatic shift in the patient's behavior in the treatment from raging to submission. At this point the interactive therapist would become quite concerned that a collusion had formed between the insistent, intrusive therapist and the compliant patient in order to block further analytic progress and to end the treatment with mutual congratulations. The interactive therapist would not view the change in the patient's demeanor as a hopeful sign or as an indication that *anything* had been worked through.

> The first analysis ended with some apparently good results: The masochistic fantasies gradually disappeared, and the patient moved from his mother's house to an apartment of his own. He began to date and had several sexually active relationships with girls of his age. During the last year of his analysis he seemed to have formed a serious relationship with a woman and was considering marriage. All this occurred *pari passu* with Kohut's firm rejection of Mr. Z.'s narcissistic expectations and his insistence that they were resistances against deeper fears connected with masculine assertiveness and competition with men. Kohut reported that the patient "seemed indeed to respond favorably to this consistent and forcefully pursued attitude on my part" (p. 8).

This clinical material can be understood in the same fashion as the material in the previous clinical paragraph. Each listening stance could hear it as further evidence for the aspects of the material that particular stance would have emphasized, as delineated in the previous two interpretive paragraphs.

> About half a year before termination, the patient reported an important dream: "*He was in a house, at the inner side of a*

> *door which was a crack open. Outside was the father, loaded with gift-wrapped packages, wanting to enter. The patient was intensely frightened and attempted to close the door in order to keep the father out*" (p. 8). The patient had many associations, involving both past and present experiences, including the transference. Kohut's interpretation centered around the patient's ambivalence toward his father, focusing on the hostility to his return and Mr. Z.'s castration fear. Kohut again emphasized the retreat from this to either a preoedipal attachment to the mother or a defensively adapted submissive or passive homosexual attitude toward the father.

We are given little detail about the associations to the dream. Kohut's interpretation arises from standard drive/conflict/defense listening. The object relations stance, especially from a Kleinian point of view, might emphasize the gift-wrapped packages with which the father is loaded down in the dream. The wish to incorporate all these packages is frightening to the patient. Depending on how closely the therapist followed Klein's theories, these packages could be thought of as part objects—breasts, penises, and so forth—or, at a more abstract level, all-good self and object representations that the patient yearned to incorporate inside himself in order to neutralize his own bad inner self and object representations.

The phenomenological approach to this dream and its associations would take the dream more at face value, focusing on the struggle between the patient and his father. The father has everything; he is loaded down with gift-wrapped packages. We are not told in the dream that these gifts are for the patient or who they are for. It is possible these are gifts that have been given to the father, thereby emphasizing his power, his genitals, and his other possessions (perhaps the mother), all of which he is potentially able to give to the patient should he wish to do so. There is a hint here of threatened penetration of the patient through the crack opening in the doorway,which the patient is attempting to close. The theme of struggle and danger is emphasized by the patient's intense fright.

The interactive point of view would carry this even further and emphasize the transference nature of this dream. In it the patient is attempting to keep from being penetrated by the therapist; the patient is in a passive, frightened, submissive homosexual attitude toward the therapist. The interactive point of view would emphasize that this relationship arose as a result of the therapist's initial stance and was fostered by his increasing assertiveness and firmness—an attitude to which the patient responded with increasingly passive and submissive compliance. So even the improvements in the patient's life represent an attempt to please the therapist and to comply with his wishes, which at the same time enables the therapy to come to an end and permits the patient to get away. Thus Mr. Z. met the analyst's expectations by suppressing his symptoms and changing his behavior to fit the appearance of normalcy as defined by what Kohut calls the analyst's "maturity morality," the apparent move from narcissism to object love.

> The termination phase of the analysis was emotionally shallow and unexciting, a joyless phase of the treatment. The analysis ended with a warm handshake and the patient's expression of gratitude. There was no contact with Mr. Z. after that for about five years, except for a brief letter three weeks after the last session containing the last payment and another expression of gratitude. The therapist met Mr. Z. accidentally on two occasions, once at the

> theater and once at a concert, and each time he was accompanied by a young woman whom he introduced to the therapist. There ensued a brief and friendly social chat.

It is difficult to assess this section of the case report because it is difficult to know how much of it is based on a retrospective sense that something was wrong; it is not clear whether at the time the therapist actually realized that something had miscarried in the treatment, for otherwise he surely would not have allowed the termination to take place so easily. The phenomenological or interactive point of view might have stressed that the patient was simply marking time until the therapy was terminated and that he had already withdrawn affectively from the treatment. Not enough material is provided for any listening stance to have picked up definitively that something had basically miscarried in the treatment, or evidence that would have been sufficient to justify trying to postpone the termination. In addition, we have no indication that the patient had any strong wish to continue the treatment at this point.

THE CASE OF MR. Z.: THE SECOND ANALYSIS

> Four and a half years later, Mr. Z. contacted Kohut again, and he appeared to be under some strain. He was still not attached to any particular woman but had had a succession of affairs and was living alone, so at least he was involved in heterosexual activity. However, like the ending of his analysis, the relationships in which he engaged were emotionally shallow and unsatisfying, even in their sexual aspect. The addictive masturbation with the sadomasochistic fantasies had recurred. He was living a joyless existence; even

> his work felt like a burden. As a matter of fact, he had to call up the sadomasochistic fantasies during intercourse with his girlfriends in order to prevent premature ejaculation and to enjoy the sexual act more keenly. What alarmed him the most was an increasing sense of social isolation.
>
> The patient continued in the first two interviews by reporting that his mother, whom he had moved away from about five years earlier, had developed a paranoid psychosis. Kohut wondered whether this was a precipitant to the patient's worsening condition and his turning again for help. Within two interviews the patient appeared to be feeling much better, and he agreed to wait until Kohut was ready in about a half a year to begin a second analysis. The patient tolerated this waiting period quite well.

At this point, Kohut, having adopted the self-psychology listening stance, entertains the hypothesis that the patient has developed an idealizing transference. I deliberately left out the self-psychological approach to the material in my discussion of the first analysis because the second analysis is based primarily on that approach, and it is presented by Kohut himself. Indeed, Kohut's purpose in detailing the two analyses of Mr. Z. is to illustrate how the adoption of the self-psychological listening stance enabled him to understand the patient in an entirely different manner than he had in the first analysis and, subsequently, to bring the second analysis to a more successful conclusion.

The drive/conflict/defense orientation would stress the importance of the mother's paranoid psychosis in Mr. Z.'s deteriorating condition after the first analysis, probably emphasizing, as Kohut speculates, the loss of an unrelinquished love object from childhood, or guilt feelings about having abandoned her and thus causing her illness, or both. In fact, the patient himself had considered these possibilities and reported some feelings of loss and guilt.

The phenomenological approach would focus on the patient's gradual deterioration after parting from the analyst, his increasing isolation and return to his preanalytic condition, and therefore would stress the loss of the analyst as an important factor in upsetting the patient's psychic equilibrium. An object relations stance would carry this further and link the loss of the analyst and the loss of the mother, immersing the patient in Klein's depressive position, which he tries unsuccessfully to resolve by isolating himself and by involving himself in a series of meaningless sexual affairs. From this point of view the patient is in danger of further disintegration toward the paranoid-schizoid position.

The interactive listening stance might focus on the unresolved transference from the first analysis. The patient left in a state of compliance, colluding with the therapist to please both of them and continuing the relationship during the interval between analyses with some very brief, pleasant superficial social interaction, while at the same time becoming increasingly depressed as a function of his frustration and repressed rage. From this listening point of view, the patient contacted the therapist in a spontaneous desperate effort to try once more to resolve the conflict between them; from Langs's (1982) extreme interactive point of view, the patient would be thought of as making one last heroic effort to heal the therapist.

> The first dream of the second analysis consisted simply of an image of a dark-haired man, whom Kohut believed from the associations to be a condensation of the camp counselor, the patient's father, and Kohut. This image, admiringly described, of a man with an impressive appearance and proud bearing, was taken as a confirmation that the patient

> had developed an idealizing transference. In his associations the patient also recalled the previously described dream of his father laden with gift packages, indicating to Kohut that the second analysis was indeed a continuation of the first one. The man in the new dream is in a rural landscape, "strong and confidence-inspiring" (p. 11). He is wearing a ring, a handkerchief protrudes from his breast pocket, and he is holding perhaps an umbrella in one hand and possibly a pair of gloves in the other.

We are given little detail about the associations to this dream, and it is often not mentioned in papers that comment on this case or in various summaries of the case. Because we have little information, there tends to be a speculative nature to the understanding of this dream; we are told only what "the associations showed" (p. 11), but the associations themselves are not disclosed, except for the brief recall of the other dream.

From the drive/conflict/defense point of view, there is some standard phallic symbolism expressed in the dream, but affectively, there is a kind of quiet neutrality about it, and a hint of a voyeuristic ambience. The prominent ring, handkerchief, umbrella, and gloves could be another edition of the gift-wrapped packages in the previous dream and could be interpreted the same way. As Kohut remarks, the manifest content of these two dreams "invites comparison" (p. 23). The object relations listening stance could focus on the almost spooky isolation of this dream man from the patient since the dream consists primarily of a picture, a visual image, although very sharp and prominent against a blurred "rural" background. This could represent some kind of a projected internal representation that the patient has not been able to reach, possibly the ego ideal, which would be consistent with Kohut's interpretation, and possibly not.

The phenomenological approach would also stress the separateness of this image and the alienated quietness of the picture—thus the lack of emotion and interaction in the dream. An interactive listening stance might read this dream as corroboration of the patient's sense of separation from the therapist and lack of resolution of the transference. Indeed, to the interactive therapist it is the representation of the analyst that is most important in this dream, and the complexity of the analyst's dress could represent a comment on the patient's experience of the analyst as aloof, distant, and perhaps narcissistic or self-preoccupied.

Actually, there are more unanswered questions about this dream than anything else, partly because of the fact that we are given few associations. For example, why does the image occur in a rural landscape? What is the meaning of the handkerchief protruding from the man's breast pocket? What about the remarkable contrast between the two dreams? The first dream portrays a dramatic and frightening situation in which two dynamic forces oppose each other without any evidence of net movement; that is, the patient is pushing the door closed against the father, who is pushing it open. In the second dream there is also no motion, but it is the result of no obvious interplay of forces; there is simply no action. From a general point of view, this second dream has a certain eerie character and an ambience of unrelatedness in contrast to the intense struggle between the father and the patient in the first dream, a struggle more characteristic of a neurosis centering on the Oedipus complex.

> Kohut reported that although he did not interfere with the patient's idealization of him, it began to subside and was replaced by a self-centered demandingness, with an inclination to react with rage if there was any misunder-

> standing—a situation similar to the beginning of the first analysis.

Kohut's self-psychological interpretation of this material was that it represented a shift from an idealizing to a mirror transference. He no longer looked upon it as defensive, but rather as a replica of a childhood condition consistent with his new theories of self psychology. To put it another way, from the point of view of the drive/conflict/defense stance, such demandingness and rage is heard as defensive and as an inevitable part of the resistance to uncovering; whereas from the self-psychological approach to listening, it is understood as a manifestation of the unfolding selfobject transference and is an expectable and desirable development in the proper analysis of patients with disorders of the self.

From an object relations point of view, the patient's verbal and behavioral communications would be heard as expressing a problem in the separation–individuation stage of development. Kohut objects to this listening stance because it does not explain the patient's chronic despair and resurgent sexual masochism. At this point he claims to have set aside "any goal-directed therapeutic ambitions" (p. 12). From the interactive point of view, this, by itself, would make a difference in the further development of the patient's material, as it would reduce the power struggle between patient and therapist. This would be true regardless of the therapist's reason for putting aside ambitions for the patient. Kohut's point is that developing the self-psychology listening stance enabled him to do this.

> The relationship to the patient's mother came into a different focus. The idealized picture of her left from the first analysis now shifted to that of a mother with intense and

> unshakable convictions that enslaved those around her and stifled independent existence. Her support and encouragement always rested on the condition "that he submit to total domination by her, that he must not allow himself any independence, particularly as concerned significant relationships with others" (p. 13). Father, son, and even the servants were strictly dominated by her. Mr. Z. realized that his father's escapade with the nurse was really a flight from the mother, and he abandoned his son to her in the process. The patient felt helplessly caught in an archaic enmeshment within the psychic organization of the mother; the loss of her as an archaic selfobject threatened him with a dissolution of himself. Transference distortions occurred as childhood memories were recovered; these did not lead to any sustained distortion of the image of the analyst, however, but usually disappeared quickly and were replaced by more childhood memories of the mother.

The self-psychological explanation of the comparative lack of transference distortion at this point is that such a lack is in the service of the progress of the treatment, because the patient cannot perceive his mother's serious pathology without perceiving his current selfobject, the analyst, as a relatively nonpathological selfobject. But a drive/conflict/defense orientation might lead to concern about this lack of transference distortion, and curiosity about whether it does not indeed have a defensive function.

An interactive therapist might ask whether the treatment has not degenerated into a simple relationship therapy in which the patient is receiving a corrective emotional experience from the relatively benign analyst; in gratitude for this, the patient feeds the analyst with clinical material that corroborates the analyst's theoretical stance. In this situation the patient has significantly more power and control than he did in the first analysis, and this increased power and control in itself, when experienced vis-à-vis the struggle with a very significant authority figure like the analyst, constitutes a corrective emotional experience when there is no resulting retaliation or destruction.

> The patient reported considerable information that demonstrated rather convincingly the pathological enmeshment between the patient and his mother. She was clearly suffering from a serious borderline personality disorder that eventually deteriorated into a paranoid psychosis after the patient moved away from her. This deterioration itself was taken as evidence, along with many of Mr. Z.'s associations and memories, of how the patient was used in the service of holding together the mother's precarious psychological structure. The patient proceeded to reveal a number of bizarre and intrusive childhood rituals involving his mother's preoccupation with his body and products, illustrating her rigid hold on and control over the patient, and forming quite a contrast to the idealized picture of her that Mr. Z. had presented in his first analysis.

Kohut argues that this material about the patient's mother was not disclosed in the first analysis because his drive/conflict/defense orientation "had become for the patient a replica of the mother's hidden psychosis, of a distorted outlook on the world to which he had adjusted in childhood, which he had accepted as reality" (p. 16). He therefore depicts the improvement from the first analysis as a "transference cure" in which the therapist unwittingly played the role of the mother in a repetitive situation that called for the patient to comply by accepting the therapist's view of the world.

It has already been mentioned that Ostow (1979), a traditional analyst, complains that Kohut simply missed the contrast between the patient's idealized picture of the mother and the raging transference reaction in the first analysis. From Ostow's drive/conflict/defense orientation, the first analysis would be described as having been ruined by the analyst's countertransference blindness rather than by his incapacity to listen from the viewpoint of self psychology. Traditional analysts like Ostow might claim that in a properly conducted psychoanalysis, the problem with the patient's mother would have emerged and been worked through, as it was in the second analysis with Kohut. In fact, Rangell (1981) insists that the "two analyses of Mr. Z." actually constituted one proper classical analysis.

Proponents of all the listening stances employed in this book could maintain that a therapist would eventually have arrived at the patient's preoedipal psychopathology and become aware of his calamitous early enmeshment with a prepsychotic mother, if their listening stances were properly employed and were not interfered with by countertransference or lack of proper training. Kohut, in contrast, argues that a shift to the theoretical listening stance of self psychology was first necessary before this vital material could emerge in a proper ambience and be heard. Whether or not this contention is accurate remains a debated issue in the psychoanalytic literature. The second analysis has a definite ring of authenticity about it, but it does not follow from the excellence of Kohut's therapeutic work that a self-psychology stance is necessary or validated. Kohut at this point in his career has become a most effective and convincing writer, but analysts of equal stature and authority protest they could have done the same therapeutic work by listening from a traditional stance.

> As the second analysis proceeded, the patient became resistive and anxious in attempting to decide "Which reality

> was real?" (p. 16). There were three realities: that of his mother, that for which the first analysis had stood, and that which presented itself in the second analysis. The deciding factor appeared to be that his mother had actually developed by this time a set of psychotic delusions that proved her outlook could not be "reality." The recognition that she was psychotic brought a sense of relief to the patient because at last there were others who could recognize that his mother's view of the world was pathological. Whether the reality of the first analysis or the reality of the second analysis was "real" centered on a reinterpretation of the sadomasochistic masturbation fantasies. Now they were understood as an attempt to obtain at least some sort of pleasure, which Kohut labels "the joyless pleasure of a defeated self" (p. 17), through self-stimulation. According to Kohut, the masturbation was now seen, not as drive-motivated, but as an attempt simply to temporarily obtain the reassurance of being alive. Other material, such as the significance of the primal scene experience, was again reinterpreted as belonging to the depression that pervaded his childhood, part of the demand to be absorbed by the mother's activities, rather than as a drive-motivated manifestation of the healthy curiosity of a growing child.

The material of the second analysis is presented in such a way as to demonstrate the self-psychological listening stance along with the case presentation; indeed that is the purpose of Kohut's paper. We have already seen how the other listening stances approached this same material in the first analysis.

> Now the patient began to discuss his father at great length. A new interpretation of the homosexual involvement was presented; it represented not a regression to the search for the phallic mother, but rather a yearning for the figure of a strong, fatherly man, perhaps the admired older brother

> Mr. Z. never had. At the crucial moment in the treatment, it became clear that a powerful, positive, unrecognized relationship had formed in childhood to his selfobject father. This was frightening, because its development required separation from the archaic self enmeshed with the selfobject mother, a self that Mr. Z. had always considered his only one. The reactivation was therefore possible in the analysis "of a hitherto unknown independent nuclear self (crystallized around an up-to-now unrecognized relationship to his selfobject father)" (p. 19).
>
> This material was accompanied by a strong transference involvement, manifested by a great need to know as much as possible about the analyst personally. Various questions that the patient asked were first interpreted as a revival of infantile curiosity about the sex life of his parents. The patient responded to this interpretation with depression and a sense of being misunderstood. Then Kohut "ventured the guess" (p. 18) that the questions represented the need for a strong father, to find out whether Kohut fit this need. This interpretation led to "a dramatic lessening" (p. 18) of the patient's depression, and the patient dropped his demanding questions and even interpreted Kohut's refusal to answer them as a sign of the analyst's strength.

This is probably the most important material of the second analysis. Kohut uses it as a confirmation of his self-psychological interpretations. The drive/conflict/defense orientation might, as Kohut initially did, treat the inquiries as representing a drive-motivated wish to be involved in the sex life of the patient's parents. From an object relations point of view, one might consider the patient's wish to identify with or even swallow up the therapist, forming a new and powerful benign introject to help the patient to deal with the destructive and pathological maternal introject. This "analytic introject" has been described from an object relations point of view, such as that of Giovacchini (1975), as a central therapeutic structure internally formed as the product of a well-conducted psychoanalysis.

A phenomenologist might think here of the work of Lacan, and especially about his concept of oedipization (see Lemaire 1981 for a summary; also Chessick 1985a, 1987a,b). As a child resolves the Oedipus complex, according to Lacan, it is born into the world of signs and symbols; thus Mr. Z.'s need to know everything about the father figure similarly might represent his reemergence into the real world from his defensive isolation. The child finds its place in the human order through this identification with the father, and if oedipization has not occurred, it remains in a state of "foreclosure" and alienation. Mr. Z.'s family picture is typical of one that Lacan says generates a state of "foreclosure," a dyadic bind with the mother.

Interactive therapists might be concerned about the patient's supplying his own interpretation of the therapist's refusal to accede to his demands as "a sign of the therapist's strength," and experiencing the refusal as "friendly firmness." The danger that this suggests both a reaction formation and further submissive compliance would be emphasized. Kohut specifically disagrees with the anticipated contention that the second analysis represented nothing but a shift to a new compliance. He cites the working through of fears of noncompliance and the joyful treatment result as militating against this contention.

Both an interactive therapist and an object relations therapist might view the transference idealization of the therapist and the father as a defense against the patient's profound rage at the father for abandoning him to the cruelty and destructiveness of the pathological mother. This view from the object relations listening stance presents one of the most fundamental disagreements between object relations theories, such as those of Kernberg, and the self psychology of Kohut. Although the patient complains about the father's weakness, at no time during either analysis is there reported a long period of the release of such rage at the father; it is the mother who emerges from the analysis with an extremely negative image. The self-psychological explanation for this is that Mr. Z. was now relinquishing the archaic self connected with the selfobject mother that he had always thought to be his only one, in preparation for the reactivation of a new independent nuclear self that would be crystallized around a hitherto unrecognized relationship to the selfobject father.

SELF-PSYCHOLOGY STANCE: ARGUMENTS AND COUNTERARGUMENTS

> The second analysis took a turn entirely different from the first analysis, moving away from hopeless rivalry with the father to a feeling of pride in him; oedipal material and conflicts did not lie hiding underneath, says Kohut, The analyst-father was experienced as strong and masculine, an image of masculine strength with which to merge temporarily as a means of firming the structure of the self.
>
> The termination was marked by a spontaneous return to the previously quoted dream from the termination of the first analysis which according to Kohut, took on a different meaning, as indicated by new, surprising associations. In contrast to the previous explanation that it involved the ambivalence of the child toward the oedipal rival, this dream is now explained as the father's sudden return, exposing the patient to the massive potential satisfaction of

> a central psychological need. It was traumatic for the patient to be offered, with overwhelming suddenness, all the psychological gifts (packages) for which he had secretly yearned. Kohut writes, "This dream deals in its essence with the psycho-economic imbalance of major proportions to which the boy's psyche was exposed by the deeply wished-for return of his father, not with homosexuality, especially not with an oedipally based reactive-passive homosexuality" (p. 23).

This material, besides illustrating the self-psychological point of view, also serves to dramatically highlight the irreconcilable differences between interpretations made on the basis of these various theoretical listening stances. From the point of view of self psychology, Mr. Z. was able to set in motion a traumatically derailed developmental sequence that involved the idealized father. According to Ornstein (1981), interpreting the father dream near termination at the end of the first analysis as representing oedipal rivalry shut off the resumption of this development, whereas the acquisition of idealized male strength through transmuting internalizations, Ornstein says, "was the central event of the second phase of the second analysis" (p. 372). Ornstein concludes that a comprehensive understanding of the mother's psychopathology and its impact on Mr. Z. became possible when the mode of listening shifted to empathy or vicarious introspection. In this mode, the self-psychology point of view focuses the analyst's attention and perception on how it feels to be the subject, rather than the target, of the patient's needs and demands, a topic emphasized by Schwaber and reviewed in the first chapter of this book. Ornstein hails this case as a demonstration that the self-psychology approach led to more accurate genetic reconstructions, a better grasp of the nature of Mr. Z.'s psychopathology, and more profound therapeutic results.

I reviewed the various discussions and objections to Kohut's interpretations of the case of Mr. Z. in a previous work (Chessick 1985a). Five years after he published the case, Kohut (1984) commented on it again, emphasizing even more the change in the atmosphere that prevailed in the two analyses. He divides the statements of others on the case into two classes: the comments of an inimical group of colleagues who claim that the first analysis was poorly conducted or that Kohut was the victim of countertransference; and the comments of a friendly group of colleagues who are essentially made uncomfortable by the suggestion that self psychologists have, somehow, a greater humaneness in their approach to patients, as allegedly demonstrated by comparing the two analyses of Mr. Z. Kohut rejects the poor-technique criticism, the countertransference criticism, and the "propaganda" criticism. He believes that his technique in the first analysis was traditional and acceptable, although he admits that perhaps some intuitively gifted analysts may have approached Mr. Z. more in the method of the second analysis. He claims that traditional analysts would not have recognized the correct interpretation of the "self-state dream" that arose in both analyses and would have been more inclined to analyze the dream as Kohut did in the initial analysis. A shift to the theory of self psychology was first necessary. A change from a focus on faulty psychic functioning to a focus on the faulty structures responsible for the faulty functioning was required before a shift in listening and interpretive technique was possible, and it was this shift that eventually enabled the understanding of the patient's pathological merger with the mother. Although Kohut admits to a certain irritability with Mr. Z. in the first analysis, he suggests that his irritability was based on his dim recognition that he was coming forward with a decisive shift in emphasis for the theory and practice of psychoanalysis.

It seems clear that one of the central changes in the ambience from the first analysis to the second analysis was in the way Kohut listened to the patient's rages. In the first analysis, all of the patient's demands and rages were viewed as resisting change and representing an unwillingness to relinquish childhood gratifications stemming from his libidinal ties to his mother. In the second analysis, these same rages and demands were seen as the expressions of a feeble self "desperately—and often hoplessly—struggling to disentangle itself from the noxious selfobject, to delimit itself, to grow, to become independent" (p. 12).

> At the end of the analysis, Kohut reported that the patient showed an impressive expanded empathy, tolerance for his parents' shortcomings, improved efficiency in his profession, and an ability to pursue his activities joyfully. He subsequently married and reported to Kohut the birth of a daughter; from a second-hand report, Kohut learned that Mr. Z.'s work was recognized as outstanding, that he was an inspiring teacher, and that he had probably made a good choice in his marital partner.

Most authors who have discussed this case agree that it seems to have had a very successful outcome. It is presented very convincingly. In some ways, Kohut's approach is foreshadowed in the work of Laing (1960). For example, following Laing's phenomenological listening approach, the patient shows a false self, characterized by compliance and an attachment to the mother, and a hidden true self, based on an idealization that maintained a bond to his father and was hidden away with the memories of his father's strength. The net effect of the treatment was to enable the patient's true self to emerge. The reason this was so difficult, as Laing would agree with Kohut, is that the true self had to remain concealed. The false self was the price the patient had to pay to preserve his mother's ministrations to him, which were necessary, of course, for his survival as a child. Here we have the "politics of the family," as Laing (1969) calls it. Thus the price of the emergence of the true self was the loss of the mother and her maternal functioning, which, from a child's point of view, is absolutely terrifying and tantamount to a catastrophe.

To my knowledge, none of the commentators on this case point out that this division between Mr. Z.'s false self and his true self could have been crystallized by the father's abandoning the family when the patient was $3\frac{1}{2}$ years old. This experience taught the patient that (1) it really was possible for a parental figure to abandon a child and that (2) he now had only one parent—his mother—so that he had to make every effort to hold on to her. From this point of view, the precipitating factor that caused the patient's neurosis to irreversibly consolidate until the time of the second analysis was his father's abandonment of him. A strong argument could be made that the patient's idealization of the father was a later formation than perhaps Kohut had thought, at least in part constructed to hide the patient's rage at this calamity. Evidence for this will be discussed shortly, but first:

> At the time the second analysis took its decisive turn and the patient's material moved toward the anxiety-ridden recovery of the strong father, another image dream was reported. The patient saw a starkly outlined image of his mother, standing with her back turned toward him. The patient described the dream as filled "with the deepest anxiety he had ever experienced" (p. 19). Associations led to the mother's icy withdrawal when the patient attempted to step toward independence and independent maleness.

> Kohut suggested that the unseen frontal view of the mother in this image represented the patient's castration anxiety, a traditional psychoanalytic interpretation which the patient rejected: "He was sure that this was not the essential source of the fear" (p. 20). The patient was unable to formulate this fear; Kohut suggested that the mother lost her face in the dream and the patient responded to this with prolonged silence and a more relaxed mood. From this Kohut concluded that the dream expressed the patient's anxiety about the mother's strength and power.

Phenomenologists would be intrigued both by the masculine-image dream that appears at the beginning of the second analysis, in which, from the description, there appears to be a full and sharp image facing the patient, and the feminine-image dream, which appears at a crucial time in this second analysis, of his mother standing with her back toward him. Again there is an eerie separation or detachment from these static images, and what seems clear is that we are dealing with expressions from a very archaic level of the unconscious mind. Object relations theorists might speculate that the appearance of this mother image represents the exchange of a now-extruded maternal introject for a benign analytic introject of Kohut. Despite its extrusion, this maternal introject retains a sense of awesome danger and power, so that at this point the situation is not yet stable, and the reintegration of the patient's personality is not yet complete. This fearful aspect of the mother is what caused the introjection in the first place, and at this point there is still the danger of reintrojection and the fear of internal destruction.

A drive/conflict/defense listening stance would produce the very castration-anxiety interpretation that Kohut first suggested, but would not be so easily satisfied with the fact that the patient brushed such interpretations aside. Here a compromise is possible, in that several levels of fear may be condensed into one intense image in this dream, ranging from the most profound fear of literal destruction or abandonment by the mother, through loss of her love, through oedipal castration anxiety, up to guilt for betraying her and turning to the father.

The interactive listening stance might hear this dream as evidence for confirmation of the previously noted concern made from the interactive point of view. It expressed suspicion about the patient's reportedly experiencing Kohut's refusal to supply personal information as a sign of friendly firmness and strength. The maternal figure standing with her back to the patient, from this listening stance, could represent the analyst's rejection of the patient's quest for infantile gratification, a turning away from a real encounter with the patient, from a real intimate relationship. And indeed, throughout this treatment, Kohut wisely maintained a traditional analytic distance from Mr. Z.; one never gets the sense that a mutually gratifying regressive friendliness ever developed. When both of the analyses were over, contact was almost entirely terminated, in accord with accepted traditional psychoanalytic procedure. The patient's longing for a more personal, intimate, emotional, and warm physical relationship, which the analyst is not permitting to develop, could also be expressed in this dream. The dream is filled with anxiety because such longings for male warmth could stir up deep, frightening homosexual yearnings or, at an even deeper level, passive longing for the maternal breast, which carries with it the danger of regression and functional collapse. Although Kohut interprets the patient's marriage after analysis as being based on picking "a partner who possessed his father's best features embedded in a matrix of femininity" (p. 26), an interactive therapist might wonder whether the chosen marital partner actually "embedded" some of Kohut's features, and even whether the patient's marriage represented an unconscious homosexual relationship with the analyst acted out in the context of an acceptable marriage situation. This, of course, would contradict the entire self-psychological interpretation of the second analysis. Although Kohut (p. 23) is aware of the possibility that Mr. Z. might have developed hopes for anal penetration by his father, which would represent obtaining male psychological strength in this passive manner, he could not find evidence in the material or in the transference for any of this. It remains an issue for debate.

> During the terminal phase, there were a few sessions during which the patient did express considerable anger as he compared Kohut to his father. Just as his father had failed him in his childhood, Kohut's first analysis had failed, and therefore he was older than he should be at the stage of development he had finally reached. This anger apparently subsided spontaneously, without comment from Kohut—or at least without comment that is reported in the paper. The anger was soon replaced by images of having a son and thoughts of getting married.

There is a remarkable parallel between the two phases of Mr. Z.'s relationship with his father and his two analyses, with a time gap between the phases of each relationship. The patient seems to have a point. Was this the opportunity for Kohut to have somehow encouraged the emergence of the patient's rage? And if he had done so, would the idealization, if it was a defensive idealization, have dropped away, in which case the happy ending of the second analysis might have been quite different? We will never know.

Listening from an interactionist point of view, Meyerson (1981) describes the successful second analysis as resting on the language offered by Kohut. Meyerson argues that Kohut helped Mr. Z. consolidate his sense of being an active agent so that expressions of rage, sexuality, assertiveness, and exhibitionism, "with an antecedent sense of his being an agent responsible for what he expressed" (p. 183), allowed the patient to consolidate his true self. Such patients, according to Meyerson, must be guided, as Kohut did for Mr. Z., to the discovery that it is neither evil nor dangerous to separate from their mothers. Thus Mr. Z. came to realize that his independent actions would not lead to subsequent physical harm to his mother, and that he would not disintegrate if he were to act separately from her. According to Meyerson, "In this manner Kohut was, in a fatherly way, explicitly encouraging the analysand to realize his potential for independence and to become more of an active agent responsible for his feelings and his actions" (p. 183).

Meyerson's implication is that the second analysis of Mr. Z. was not a classical psychoanalysis, and that various departures from the more normative approach were necessary. I think Kohut would disagree with this and deny that he made any such departures; what was different was the listening stance employed in the second analysis, and this listening stance subsequently affected the nature of the interpretations. It is important to keep in mind, though, that the basic therapeutic technique need not be modified or changed in any way as a function of the particular listening stance used at any given time. All of the cases presented in this book are very difficult, and the value of having five alternative listening channels is in gathering as complete an understanding as possible of the patient's material so that the interpretations and reconstructions that are offered to the patient are as accurate as possible.

7

LISTENING TO THE "DIFFICULT" PATIENT

FREUD WOULD SAY that one's acceptance or rejection of traditional psychoanalysis stands or falls on the acceptance or rejection of the approach used by Arlow (Schwaber 1985) to a very difficult patient, an approach stressing consistent focus on the central role of the patient's psychic reality. Arlow (1985) believes that after the age of 6 or 7, every person has some sort of repetitive fantasy activity that is typical and unique for that person. It represents how the individual has attempted to integrate and resolve conflicts arising from the various experiences of the earliest years of life. Our conscious fantasy life is derived from certain basic drives that are organized in the form of core unconscious fantasies, and these unconscious fantasies exert a persistent influence against which the data of current perception are perceived, registered, interpreted, remembered, and responded to. Thus in therapy the psychoanalytic listening approach searches for the vicissitudes of the dominant elements of the patient's unconscious fantasies reflected in derivatives that appear in the transference and in the patient's communications. These derivatives determine how the individual misperceives, misinterprets, and misresponds to the data of perception.

Arlow believes these central unconscious fantasies to be so important that they determine in their derivative manifestations the patient's symptoms, character, life history, object relations, and even creative endeavors. Therefore, the decisive step Freud took from his early theory that neuroses were caused by literal sexual abuse of children during the first few years of life, to his focus on the central role of sexual fantasies that had a psychic reality in the patient's unconscious, is carried to its logical conclusion by the work of Arlow and is manifest in his approach to psychoanalytic listening. Arlow's presentation (Schwaber 1985) is one of the best examples of professional psychoanalytic listening in the current literature, a contention that I will support by my annotations and commentary. Arlow presents material from the first two sessions with a very difficult patient indeed.

THE FIRST SESSION

> "The patient was a young unmarried woman who was referred to me recently when her doctor became physically incapacitated. She had been seeing him twice a week for somewhat over four years. The patient had had my name for several weeks before she called me. When she did call, she said she was going out of town and would call again on

> her return. She called me ten days later and it seemed very difficult to arrange a time, but finally a mutually acceptable date was agreed upon" (Schwaber 1985, pp. 103–104).

Freud, in his papers on technique, warns us about patients who wish to delay before beginning the treatment; he claims that when the day to begin arrives, such patients seldom appear. He was almost right in this case.

> "On the day of the appointment she arrived fifteen minutes late. She had forgotten to get off the bus at the proper corner" (Schwaber 1985, p. 104).

Late arrival to the initial consultation due to a parapraxis is a common mark of a difficult patient; the ego functioning of such a patient is immediately called into question. For example, it is not unusual for a schizophrenic patient to begin therapy in this fashion. Patients are often most anxious at their first encounter with a strange psychotherapist, however, and tend to show themselves in their worst state of functioning because of this anxiety. The therapist can draw no definite conclusions at this point, except that when this patient's ego is laboring badly some kind of disruptive behavior may occur. Also, the therapist should make a mental note that the therapist–patient relationship will always be endangered because of this.

> "The patient was a woman in her mid-twenties, well spoken, fairly attractive, alert, vivacious, and ingratiating. Talking to her revealed that she was obviously of very superior intelligence. Some difficulties, however, began to appear almost immediately. Ordinarily I begin by asking a few questions . . . about age, occupation, marital status,

> education, family, any serious illnesses, and any history of previous psychotherapy. This time I did not get very far. The patient spoke clearly, but in obsessive detail, about nonessentials. It was difficult to budge her from the direction she chose to follow" (Schwaber 1985, p. 104).

This tangle between the therapist trying to get specific information about basic identifying and historical data and the patient thwarting the therapist's effort by the recitation of endless and tangential trivia is not an uncommon clinical situation. It suggests what Langs (1978), using the interaction model, has called the establishment of a type C field—a holding or static bipersonal field in which the patient presents boring manifest content repeatedly, regardless of what the therapist may comment or how he or she intervenes. In object relations terms, the patient is engaging in negative projective identification, placing emptiness and confusion into the therapist. From a traditional ego psychology or structural point of view, the patient is for some defensive reason obfuscating the initial data-gathering situation.

If this is accompanied by a peculiar "feel"—of the patient both being there and not being there—as described by Pao (1983), the diagnosis of schizophrenia should be considered. An extreme and dramatic clinical example of this is presented by Laing (1968), who convincingly demonstrates how the responses of a schizophrenic patient to questions from Kraeplin in an interview conducted in front of a group of doctors, and labeled by Kraeplin as making no sense at all, actually constituted a mocking caricature of the interviewer (summarized in Chapter 3).

> "Finally I decided to relinquish the lead entirely to her. First she spoke about feeling depressed and about her difficulty

> in getting on with men. She kept referring to two men she had been seeing, switching quickly and quietly from one to the other without identifying them in any specific way. Finally I asked her if she could identify each one at least by his name, so I could keep the two of them separate in my mind" (Schwaber 1985, p. 104).

Her way of reference to the boyfriends constitutes typical evidence for a type C field producing confusion in the therapist, which may be thought of as stemming from a negative projective identification as described by Bion and Klein, if one wishes to tune in on that channel.

> "On her own she turned to give me some information about her family" (Schwaber 1985, p. 104).

This "turn" to giving such information indicates that the patient is actually in better contact with reality than she pretends to be—she knows this is an initial psychiatric interview—and it militates against the diagnosis of schizophrenia and toward the diagnosis of a borderline or otherwise "difficult" patient. What she is doing is tormenting the therapist, teasing him, taking control of the treatment, and presenting everything in her own way.

> "Her father is a self-made man who overcame great hardships. In her early upbringing, women were considered of no account. . . . From this, she turned to a meticulously detailed and elaborately recited account of the onset of her menses. This subject took up almost the entire remainder of the interview. . . . There were serious endocrinological, metabolic, dermatological, arthritic, and other difficulties, and these had been variously diagnosed by different doctors . . . in the end it seemed she accepted one man's

> diagnosis but followed the other man's treatment" (Schwaber 1985, pp. 104–105).

This oscillation between "authorities" is further support for the idea that the patient's essential concern is one of manipulation, devaluation, and control rather than one of schizophrenic confusion.

> "On the one hand I felt deeply moved by the overwhelming suffering that so young a girl had to experience at such a crucial period in her life; on the other, however, I detected a certain challenging bitterness in her recital to me. The total effect upon me was, 'What a welcome to womanhood!' " (Schwaber 1985, p. 105).

Clearly this constitutes a master stroke of psychoanalytic listening, analogous to a superb move by a master chess player. Using evenly hovering attention in a difficult and frustrating interview situation, the therapist is able to form an empathic identification with the patient and detect her essential message. He is able to remain close to the clinical data and yet not become entangled in the manifest content.

This clinical situation also offers a good example of how the less experienced or unanalyzed therapist might react differently to such a patient, perhaps getting into a quarrel about the diagnosis and treatment of her organic complaints, or even trying to defend the doctors, or authoritatively insisting upon her giving certain details of the case history or upon clarification; this undoubtedly would have led to a bitter and even angry exchange, with the patient being labeled as "borderline" and perhaps "untreatable." The power struggle exacerbated by an exchange of this kind could well result in the patient's either stamping out of the treatment session angrily, or failing ever to appear again.

The crucial point illustrated here is Arlow's immediate listening orientation to the patient's past, utilizing evenly hovering attention in his traditional Freudian search for important fundamental unconscious infantile fantasies. These fantasies crucially determine the adult's subsequent behavior, thinking, and life experience. *This listening stance, the psychoanalytic stance, is a fundamental principle to be followed in the technique and practice of psychoanalytic listening. The application in a consistent fashion of this principle to all manifest content provided by the patient is the single most important mark that differentiates the experienced well-analyzed psychotherapist from the beginner.*

> "The patient was unswerving in her determination to give the details . . . it was clear that she was going to tell the story her way and I was just going to have to listen. Every once in a while, thoughts of conflict with her brother intruded into her discussion, although the patient feels that she has no problem in this area whatsoever. Nonetheless, ideas of competition and retaliation kept recurring" (Schwaber 1985, p. 105).

Although the patient produces confusion in the mind of the therapist, leaving the therapist dazed, devalued, and controlled, it is still possible that an early formulation can take place in the therapist's mind utilizing the structural model to explain the manifest content, including the patient's behavior, on the basis of childhood experiences and unconscious fantasies. The expert therapist, when confronted with a patient who is obviously speaking under great stress and with much pressure of speech and circumlocution, sometimes must allow the patient to tell his or her story in his or her own way, quietly listening with more or less evenly hovering attention. Hypotheses about the appearance of possible derivatives of childhood experiences and unconscious fantasies gradually form in the mind of the carefully listening therapist.

> "At the end of the session I told her that I thought it would be important to know something of what happened in her treatment with her previous therapist . . . she replied by describing at great length what a wonderful physician she thought he was, but she could not give any of the details of the treatment at the time or what she had learned. However, she did make reference to a number of other doctors she had consulted before and after her previous therapist, for purposes of engaging in psychotherapy. All of these comments were disparaging. At the end of the session, I told her that at the next meeting it would be useful if we could begin by discussing what she had gotten from her treatment with Dr. X." (Schwaber 1985, pp. 105–106).

A patient's inability to give any details of the previous treatment or what she had learned about herself in four years of psychotherapy, coupled with high praise for her previous doctor, is quite paradoxical and is a not uncommon ominous mark of a "difficult" patient. Also clearly illustrated here is the important principle of always listening for allusions to the therapist contained in the patient's manifest material; these allusions are a prophetic commentary on the transference that is to follow. One should always listen to such allusions in the early interviews and try to predict future transference manifestations. If such predictions turn out to be wrong, it is incumbent on the therapist to ask why; perhaps the therapist has listened incorrectly. If this is true, the therapist must carry out self-exploration.

This is one of the most powerful arguments against Gill's (1982) notion that transference is primarily a reaction of the patient to the here-and-now of the therapist–patient interaction. It seems clear in this case that the patient is bringing a "transference readiness" to the first session before she knows anything of significance about the new therapist; this is a common clinical situation. Gill, in the discussion that follows the published case, disagrees, and argues that Arlow did indeed influence the material. Here one must choose between two directly opposing viewpoints.

THE SECOND SESSION

> "The next consultation was held a week later. This time the patient was sixteen minutes late. She had walked right past the door of my building and had kept on going for about seven or eight minutes before she realized her mistake. When I asked if she had some problem with lateness, she said, 'Sometimes' " (Schwaber 1985, p. 106).

This illustrates the extraordinary patience and tolerance that is required in the treatment of difficult patients; in fact, the capacity to treat such patients and their very treatability by the psychoanalytic method is limited by the particular therapist's capacity for tolerance and patience with disparaging and depreciating and frustrating behavior on the part of the patient. A more appropriate intervention than asking her if she had some problem with lateness at this point, beside asking what had happened (as Arlow did), might have been to ask the patient why she thought she had come late to both sessions.

An alternative at this point would have been to say nothing as yet about it except to ask her why she was late, because one might prefer not to make interventions about patterns of behavior until they are well established, and this was only the second session. Often, since patients are so anxious at the beginning of therapy, they may come late or even miss some sessions at the beginning, and this gradually drops away by itself as they become more comfortable. Early interventions carry the danger of leading to a quarrel about coming on time and place the therapist in a nonanalytic authoritarian stance of marking the patient "tardy" and responding to manifest content.

> "Then I asked her if she remembered my suggestion at the end of the last session about how we should begin this one. She looked entirely blank. . . . I reminded her that I was interested in finding out what happened in her treatment with Dr. X." (Schwaber 1985, p. 106).

So much for active interventions and confrontations at the beginning of treatment with an anxious or difficult patient! The therapist recovers himself by reminding her what he said, avoiding an argument about whether she can be urged to remember it or whether he said it at all—which would be a typical beginner's mistake.

> "She made some vague sign of recognition and then proceeded to give a detailed account of her relationship with her boyfriend, A., with no mention whatsoever of the question I had put to her. She stopped after about ten minutes and said, 'You know, I am not telling you what you asked me about' " (Schwaber 1985, pp. 106–107).

This spontaneous statement on the part of the patient is precisely what the experienced therapist looks for in assessing the ego function of the patient. It represents the patient's capacity for self-observation and indicates that she has some; it renders at least the possibility that, with patience, this individual is amenable to treatment by the psychoanalytic method because she has some remaining observing ego function.

> "I told her to proceed in whatever way she felt was best for her. . . . The story that she gave of her love life was meticulously described insofar as insignificant details were concerned . . . he has proposed and she has proposed: the relationship has been on and off, on and off, on and off. They never can get together on a decision at the same time. Listening to her account, I had the thought, 'This is a kind of cat-and-mouse game' " (Schwaber 1985, p. 107).

His thought is an excellent example of the product from employing Freud's concept of psychoanalytic listening. It requires the willingness to suspend judgment and suspend attention and let the patient stir up in the mind of the therapist whatever associations to the message her unconscious wishes to transmit. This thought must be validated by listening further, which enables the therapist to discover similar patterns in relationships. Again it is to be used as a cue or clue for what to look for in further careful listening for derivatives of an unconscious early childhood fantasy.

> "In the interim she had seen a number of other men and followed a similar pattern with them. She gets involved with them and at a certain point receives a proposal of marriage. At such time she is beset with doubt, and soon afterward finds some reason to precipitate a break-up. Each time she has found that she is really interested in her

> original boyfriend, A. . . . At one point A. received an offer from a prestigious professional firm from out of town. It was a job that he had wanted. When it was offered to him, he accepted it immediately by phone. A. then informed my patient that he had accepted the job and now they could get married and go off together to the other city. The patient became furious. How could he have accepted the offer without consulting her? Her anger arose despite the fact that she had been encouraging him to take the position if it was offered. She explained that, considering he had accepted a position without consulting her, she could only anticipate a life where she would be denigrated, disregarded, and not consulted on any of the important decisions.
>
> At that point I observed, 'Then you felt that this was a good time to break off the relationship?' 'Oh, on the contrary,' she replied. . . . No other man has the same appeal for her as A. She does not know why; she had raised the question with her previous therapist" (Schwaber 1985, pp. 107–108).

The intervention reflects the therapist's confusion about how to proceed in the face of the patient's apparent irrationality.

> "Then she said to me, 'I think I'm so attached to him because he was the first man that I had sexual relations with. Do you think this could have anything to do with it?' " (Schwaber 1985, p. 108).

This challenge may be understood as the manifestation of an archaic transference (Gedo 1977, Gunther 1984), in which the patient is demanding an immediate response from the therapist. It is fraught with difficulties. If the therapist is silent, the patient becomes enraged at his "rudeness" in not offering an answer to her question. But obviously *any* definitive answer to the question, based on the previous material, would be the wrong answer and would be met with objections, denials, and possibly also even an irrational enraged situation, again getting the patient labeled as "borderline."

Perhaps a validation of the difficulty such an archaic transference challenge poses to the therapist is found in Arlow's case report, because he never tells us how he responded to this challenge. Furthermore, he breaks off a description of the patient's material at this point and enters into an interesting theoretical discussion, which, to say the least, is surely much less anxiety provoking for the therapist. He does not break off entirely at this point, however, but adds one more paragraph that is a kind of summary of the situation to that time:

> "I want to point out three reactions that I had while the patient was talking. First, I was aware of becoming annoyed. I amused myself by thinking that, in my younger days, when I was possessed of greater therapeutic zeal and enthusiasm, I would have tried to pursue various details in which I was interested. This time I just permitted the patient to continue talking" (Schwaber 1985, p. 108).

A depth self-analysis of this characteristic defense against annoyance by amusing one's self might be that Arlow soothed himself by a sublimated fantasy about his vigorous youth, a time in which his already reported rage and destructiveness at such a frustrating, annoying patient would be transformed into "therapeutic zeal," a not uncommon countertransference reaction. A translation might be, "If I were not such a kindly old doctor but the potent young man I was once, I would show you who was the cat and who was the mouse." It is very difficult for us to admit to ourselves that we would like to tear a patient to pieces, since this collides with our ego ideal of being helpful physicians.

> "In addition, I noted my ironic reaction, my thought, 'Welcome to womanhood,' and the metaphor that came to my mind to describe the way in which she interacted with the various men in her life, namely, a cat-and-mouse game" (Schwaber 1985, p. 108).

Arlow's "ironic reaction" cannot be understood unless we remember that irony also contains a hostile component—but there is also an empathic component in his thought. Similarly, one should remember that the "cat-and-mouse game," when translated into reality, is actually cruel and deadly! Anyone who has watched a cat chase, capture, tease, torment, and destroy a mouse will remember this clearly.

DISCUSSION

Arlow correctly perceived the transference, which was brought to him "without my having done anything except answer the telephone" (Schwaber 1985, p. 116)—although Gill (1982) might wonder what he said over the telephone. Indeed, in the discussion Gill suggests that the trouble setting up the first appointment time as reported represents already a cat-and-mouse game. In my supervisory experience, quite a bit more gets said over the telephone before the first session that can alter the transference for years, but in all fairness Arlow cannot be suspected of such mistakes. For Arlow—and I agree—the transference was a carryover from the previous doctor, and again we do not know what the interpersonal relationship between the patient and her previous doctor was like; the patient, on the one hand, describes it as wonderful, but on the other hand, she can remember nothing of her treatment. So something was certainly wrong.

In addition, we know that the treatment broke up because the doctor became physically incapacitated, and certainly substantial exploration would be necessary to discover the effect of this on a patient who had been seeing him twice a week for four years. Such an effect would be considerable and could by itself account for the patient's overwhelming need to control the therapy so that further disappointments would not devastate her again. Listening to this material from an empathic point of view, i.e., a self-psychology stance, would stress the effect of the previous doctor's probably unexpected incapacity, with a disruption of the treatment beyond his control, in determining this patient's apparent "borderline" presentation, and rightly so.

Another approach to this patient could be from the sociocultural phenomenological orientation, in which we could easily see how her childhood description of the disparagement of women in her milieu might have produced a low self-image, considerable rage, and the desire for being primarily a vengeful person who gains the upper hand over the coveted man. A classical interpretation of this would be "penis envy," but a sociocultural interpretation would stress not only the family's overt disparagement of women, but the whole cultural influence producing in women this sense of an inferiority, which is especially painful to intelligent superior women like the patient.

Arlow, however, takes a Freudian orientation to this material with which I completely agree as the primary channel of listening. He attempts to transform his intuitive thoughts through a cognitive process that will lead to precise interpretations,

> ". . . observing how certain ideas were repeated and how a similar theme ran through them, recognizing the contiguity and sequence in which the ideas appeared in the patient's mind and finally how they converged into two or three major ideas suggesting hostility towards physicians who had hurt her and upon whom she wished to take vengeance. In her fantasy, she wished to avenge herself in kind. Since she experienced defloration as a castration, she wanted to do the same to men, especially A. . . . Freud had already described patients of this type. In a paper entitled, 'The Taboo of Virginity' (1918a), . . . Freud noted that certain women remain emotionally bound to the first man with whom they have intercourse. The bond, however, is not one of affection, but of hostility" (Schwaber 1985, p. 117).

This is not quite an accurate review of Freud's remarks because what Freud actually said in later papers on femininity was that the bond begins as an affectionate one based on the imago of the father and then gradually shifts to an ambivalent one based on the imago of the mother. At any rate, according to Freud, the woman cannot give up the tie to the man who deflowered her because she has not yet exacted the full measure of the vengeance she wishes to wreak upon him.

Based on this listening, Arlow plans the strategy of the treatment, in which a hierarchy of interpretations are to be given in what he considers to be a rational manner:

> "The patient must first be made aware of the hostility implicit in her behavior, of her sense of having been injured in an anatomical way, of the special role that the man who

> deflowered her played in this pattern of reactions, and of the unconscious fantasy of having been castrated during defloration and of exacting vengeance. Ultimately, at each one of these phases some opportunity will arise to demonstrate to the patient how her interaction with the analyst is influenced by these ideas. This is what constitutes the interpretation of the transference. The essential principal of the entire psychotherapeutic approach, however, is to demonstrate to the patient the persistent effect of the unconscious wishes that originated during childhood, but that continue to intrude upon her current, adult mental life and behavior" (Schwaber 1985, pp. 117–118).

I (Chessick 1982b, 1983a) completely agree with Arlow's plea for formal psychoanalysis for such "difficult" patients. In psychotherapy the relative infrequency of sessions permits a greater intrusion of current reality into the clinical data, so that it becomes difficult for the therapist to perceive and for the patient to pursue the continuity of the themes in the material. Thus the appropriate treatment for borderline and difficult patients still remains essentially psychoanalytic if the patient is at all tolerant of such an approach. In fact, sometimes patients who are intolerant of the psychoanalytic approach with one therapist are able to tolerate it with a therapist of a different personality type, so that a failure to succeed in psychoanalytic therapy with one therapist does not by itself mean that the patient is not amenable to psychoanalytic psychotherapy.

RESPONDING TO ARCHAIC TRANSFERENCE DISRUPTIONS

The problem in the treatment of the borderline or difficult patient lies in the extreme stress it places on the therapist to deal with disruptions, acting out, archaic transference challenges, and the many incessant reality problems that keep impinging on the patient's chaotic life. In the hands of a skilled therapist, there is no reason that most of these patients cannot be held in the psychoanalytic situation and treated appropriately. The great danger of distorting during psychoanalytic listening with the difficult patient lies in the tremendous temptation to respond to the frustration and devaluation from such patients by shifting away from a concentration on early infantile unconscious fantasies and themes to various aspects of the manifest content.

In the early listening process with such patients, the therapist should try to remain tuned into an empathic approach as much as possible, but also provide for himself or herself a continuous silent monitoring of the latent material in terms of both drive/conflict/defense and object relations/structure theories. At the beginning one may allow the patient to cling to inexact interpretations borrowed from sociocultural or other orientations—or from previous therapists. But even though these may have some validity, the primary problem, if there is to be a real understanding of the patient's material, is to unearth the precise formative infantile unconscious fantasies and experiences that constitute the unique individuality of the particular patient and profoundly influence the entire course of the patient's future life. This is the fundamental principle of Freud's psychoanalysis.

The question of how to respond to archaic transference challenges, such as the one offered by this patient, is very thorny in some cases; it would not pose an overwhelming problem at this point in this case. In response to her challenging question quoted above, it would be a mistake to maintain a stony silence, as this would produce a raging intersubjective field that would eventually be labeled "borderline" and "untreatable" (see Brandchaft and Stolorow 1984). On the other hand, it would be narcissistic countertransference acting out to give the patient a definitive answer to her question, even though this might provide her with direct gratification.

In the management of difficult patients, only provide direct gratification when forced to do so in order to preserve the therapy, and even then there is a limit to the direct gratification that it is possible to provide without destroying the treatment situation. This is discussed most poignantly by Freud (1905) in his postscript to the case of Dora. The rule of abstinence should be followed as much as possible even with difficult patients, and the therapist should not step out of the analytic stance any more than is absolutely necessary. It goes without saying that the therapist should *never* step out of an ethical stance regardless of the circumstances, as this is always countertransference acting out on the part of the therapist and always contraindicated. Surely it is not necessary to remind therapists of the ethics involved and the responsibilities entailed in taking on the treatment of another human being. This has been discussed repeatedly elsewhere and outlined in the ethical standards of the American Psychiatric Association and the American Medical Association.

A suitable response to this patient's archaic transference challenge would have been to answer her sudden question at the end of the second session:

> "I think I'm so attached to him because he was the first man that I had sexual relations with. Do you think this could have anything to do with it?" (Schwaber 1985, p. 108).

with a statement that I hardly knew her and I did not know whether or not her attachment to this man was related to her sexual relations with him. One might add that one hoped in subsequent sessions to get a better understanding of the situation; perhaps the therapist and the patient together could come to some acceptable answer to her question. The point in this response would be to avoid wild analysis, to avoid playing the role of the authority figure, and, above all, to appeal to her observing ego to form an alliance with the therapist for the purpose of studying her psychological situation and arriving at a better understanding of her plight. *This is a major task at the beginning of psychoanalytic psychotherapy with any patient.*

It should be clear that our responses to our patients and our formulations and plans for the strategy of their treatment rest basically on our capacity for psychoanalytic listening from the very first contact with the patient, as well as our capacity to remain in a consistent psychoanalytic listening stance throughout the vicissitudes and disruptions that constitute the treatment, no matter how difficult.

EIGHT

LEARNING TO LISTEN

IN THIS CHAPTER I will clarify and sharpen the focus of the very special psychoanalytic listening stance required in order to effectively tune in to the patient's unconscious communications. This listening stance must be painstakingly learned under careful supervision. In my view this is by far the most difficult task that must be mastered if the novice in psychotherapy is to become truly empathic and sensitive in dyadic relationships, a unique expertise that marks the psychoanalytic psychotherapist as a professional.

Although it is extremely difficult to learn how to listen to a patient in a psychoanalytic empathic mode, and even more difficult to teach it, this is obviously the first step required if an "empathic resonance" is to be developed between the patient and the therapist. Wolf (1983) emphasizes this empathic resonance as a "powerful tool" for both the exploration of the arts and the understanding of creativity. Furthermore, he paraphrases Kohut's depiction of "how the empathic resonance with the analyst eventually leads to the analysand's discovery of empathic resonance in the most human aspects of his or her environment and to the development of a capacity to seek out available selfobjects in the social matrix of the surround" (p. 504). Thus, for self psychologists, empathic psychoanalytic listening and consequent reciprocal empathic resonance is conceived of as a method of gathering data, as a tool for understanding communications from the arts, and as a direct therapeutic contribution. This is the thesis of Kohut's (1984) book; even if one does not agree with his claims for empathy, at the very least it is clear that empathic listening and understanding must form the basis of any effective psychotherapeutic intervention, regardless of one's theoretical listening stance. Otherwise we have the countertransference-based flounderings of the "wild analyst."

CASE EXAMPLE

> An obsessive young man was having trouble with his professional aspirations because of a learning block. He was in psychotherapy with a "young analyst." The treatment was working, and the patient began to talk in realistic terms about resuming his education, for his learning block had become less disturbing. The therapist agreed that he was ready for this step, but to the therapist's surprise, the patient became depressed in response to his statement of

> agreement and said, "I think I must stop treatment first. You stand in my way." This episode was discussed in supervision, and the student therapist was asked *exactly* what he had said. His reply was, "I'll back you up."

Neither the therapist nor the supervisor in this particular vignette, as it is reported by Bruch (1974, pp. 87–89), show depth-psychological understanding of the interchange. The unconscious pivot of an obsessive-compulsive neurosis is a regression to anal-sadistic concerns; thus, in the treatment of an obsessive-compulsive neurotic male patient, especially if the therapist is male and says to the patient, "I'll back you up," the therapist may very well expect the patient to decide to leave treatment and to reply, "You stand in my way."

A statement like "I'll back you up" is often unconsciously perceived by very disturbed patients with homosexual and anal-sadistic concerns as the threat or offer of anal-sadistic penetration. This contention is supported by typical military and federal penitentiary experience (including my own), for example, where such a phrase is commonly used to connote either the offer or threat of heterosexual sadistic penetration or homosexual anal-sadistic assault. Propositions that hint of anal sadism to such patients commonly lead to talk about stopping treatment. In Freud's (1909) case, discussed in Chapter 5, the patient broke off and got up from the couch when he began to describe the anal-sadistic rat torture.

As soon as such subtle innuendos and connotations are discussed, we are out of the beginner-therapist stage. Basic texts on psychotherapy tell one to be considerate to the patient, to politely greet the patient, and all that (Chessick 1974), but soon the student reaches the point at which more than a relationship is necessary. To move intensive psychotherapy forward, the student therapist must learn how to achieve a depth understanding of patients. This in turn rests on developing the capacity to receive and understand communications from the patient's (and one's own) unconscious. Many psychotherapists today never get beyond the beginner-therapist stage. They stop at this point, concluding their training after having studied only basic procedure books and lectures that any good student in a health-related profession could (and should) read.

Another way to look at the intervention just described is as an example of the typical confusion of empathy with specific technical interventions, described by Schwaber (1981b). As she points out,

> Patients with more serious pathology seem to require some more active responsiveness on our part . . . we may feel we ought to say or do something more immediate. . . . Such an intervention has often been taken as synonymous with an empathic response . . . It is, then, not the analyst's direct action—whether or not it is taken—but always the search for meaning of the patient's quests, taking cognizance of its dynamic imperative, which would utilize the work of empathy. [p. 128]

Schwaber's views were discussed at length in Chapter 1, and the reader may wish to review that discussion before continuing this chapter.

CAN READING HELP?

Pieper (1987) wrote:

> Teaching does not consist in a man's making public talks on the results of his meditations, even if he does so *ex cathedra* before a

> large audience. Teaching in the real sense takes place only when the hearer is reached—not by dint of some personal magnetism or verbal magic, but rather, when the truth of what is said reaches the hearer as true. . . . And being taught is something else again from being carried away, and something else again from being dominated by another's intellect. . . . Teaching therefore presupposes that the hearer is sought out where he is to be found. [p. 32]

What the teacher must do is to help the student therapist arrive at a convincing and deeper understanding of patients, get a greater sense of the rich depth of the human mind, and, above all, develop a grasp of the powerful intrapsychic forces that are inherent in *every* dyadic relationship. In attempting to become sensitive to the intrapsychic aspects of how interventions are experienced by the patient, the therapist must be immersed in something that is much more controversial and that requires a considerably greater imagination and knowledge of the literature—both psychiatric and humanistic—if the proper associations are to occur to the therapist. When a teacher presents this idea to student therapists, however, it produces a certain anxiety, because when exposed to the strange, primary-process world of unconscious intrapsychic pathology, unanalyzed listeners react with all their own defenses. The ego is driven by discomfort to reduce the anxiety invariably evoked by the mysterious, the horrible, the unacceptable—an uncanny experience best produced in art by such stories as those of Edgar Allen Poe.

Numerous books and articles usually serve, along with case presentations, as a starting point for student seminars. Students today are reading less and less, which is unfortunate indeed, and it is the task of the seminar leader to guide the reading selections and to use them as a springboard for discussion and learning.All too often the difficult craft of teaching such seminars is voluntarily undertaken by a tired clinician or by a new and inexperienced faculty member. Youthful zeal and clinical experience, although quite important, do not by themselves ensure successful teaching, especially in such an elusive and personal discipline as that of intensive psychotherapy.

Reading on the subject should properly begin with at least a brief study of the person who brought the idea of intrapsychic pathology into the foreground of Western thought, Nietzsche (for an introduction and a list of pertinent selections for psychotherapists, see Chessick 1983b). Next, there is no substitute for reading, directly and repeatedly, the unparalleled prose of Freud, who made a "science" out of psychoanalysis—or who at least tried to give it scientific respectability, to make rational laws of the irrational (Chessick 1980a, 1984). After a thorough grounding in Freud, to challenge the imagination students should read Melanie Klein (for introductions, see especially Grosskurth 1986, Segal 1974), and, to sample the most extreme extension of her thought, they should gain an acquaintance with the work of Bion (for an introduction see Grinberg, Sor, and de Bianchedi 1977). These works depict the aggressive and libidinal intrapsychic concerns of modern humans. A complementary approach, with focus on the narcissistic concerns of modern humans, appears in Lasch's (1978) *The Culture of Narcissism*, which is a painless preparation for Kohut's (1971) *The Analysis of the Self* and his later works (1977, 1978, 1984). Without an understanding of complex authors like Kohut and Bion, the ground of psychoanalytic listening will seem magical and mystical indeed. Greenberg and Mitchell (1983) place these drive/conflict/defense, object relations, and self-psychological orientations in reasonable order for seminar study. Selections from Jaspers (1954, 1972), and Gill's publications (1982, 1988) along with Stone's book (1961), are good starting points for the phenomenological and the interactive approaches, respectively. Of course, there are many books and articles on these theoretical stances, and each seminar leader will have favorites to recommend. I have mentioned only a few of the usual choices.

It is no accident that the problem of how to listen properly in intensive psychotherapy confronts us with a basic issue that is also the biggest preoccupation of continental philosophy, which phrases it in terms of the human as constituting a "transcendental/empirical doublet." This depiction was coined by the author-philosopher Michel Foucault (1970), whom very few American psychiatrists have read. His complex style deters some, but he produced several books on psychiatry and on the literature of psychiatry that are very well known among philosophers; examples include *Madness and Civilization* (1973), *History of Sexuality* (vol. 1, 1980), and *Discipline and Punish* (1975). Continental philosophy has recognized that humans cannot be reduced to something that compares with a machine or a "thing" and still be understood. Every effort to do this has embedded itself in a paradox, as Foucault (1970) convincingly demonstrates in *The Order of Things*. There is *more* to a human than there is to a machine or an apparatus or a computer or any other thing. Elsewhere I have reviewed aspects of Foucault's thought pertinent to the practice of psychotherapy and psychiatry (Chessick 1987b); for an excellent introduction to Foucault's work (but difficult for those unfamiliar with continental philosophy), see Dreyfus and Rabinow (1982).

At the simplest level, we work in psychiatry with the human as a chemical and physiological organism, and we try to ameliorate various disorders by using chemicals and electric shock and carbon dioxide inhalation and everything imaginable—even whirling chairs, immersion into cold baths, needle showers, and so on, endlessly throughout the historyof psychiatry. What we do in all this is to deal with symptoms of the disorder. As is the case in DSM-IIIR, the symptoms are conceived of as constituting and defining the disorder. Thus the treatment of the disorder is the treatment of the symptoms. Any good internist can be taught to do it; one does not require much understanding of humans to make such prescriptions.

Some well-intentioned psychiatrists and other psychotherapists have suggested, "Let us use a decent, sensible approach with these difficult people. We should try common-sense therapy, explanation, education, rational therapy, cognitive therapy; we should appeal to the patient's capacity for reason." That is fine, except that it does not produce any basic change in the patient. These methods are best conceptualized as a form of mental behavior therapy, or suggestion, or more technically, manipulation of the transference. Sometimes, of course, that is all that can be done. In a careful consideration of this issue, Gill (1988) produced a very interesting and controversial paper, differentiating psychoanalysis from psychotherapy, not on the traditional grounds of use of the couch, frequency of sessions, and so on, but on the basis of whether the curative element in the treatment rests primarily on the identification and interpretation of the transference or on an unanalyzed but corrective relationship.

In the psychoanalytic mode, we attempt to reach a depth beyond the level of symptoms. The problem that we face in doing intensive psychoanalytic psychotherapy is, How do we enter into the world of another person to such an extent that we can actually alter the way that person has learned to perceive, and subsequently to deal with, the world? How do we change the mind of the patient (Goldberg 1987b)? That is much harder, and to attempt it we have to be able to listen to the patient at a "transcendental" or empathic level as well as at an empirical level. This is a very difficult concept for students to grasp, especially if they have little background in philosophy or the humanities, so I will now offer some illustrations and discussion in the hope of clarifying what is often presented in murky and tortuous prose by continental writers.

WILFRED BION

A psychoanalyst who thought and wrote in a rather flowery and metaphorical way, Bion (1963, 1967, 1977) said that each of us is the "O." By an "O," he meant the individual human as one really is in one's true depth. Bion describes the analyst listening to the patient's free associations, listening to the patient's material, looking at the patient, watching how the patient conducts himself or herself, and watching for slips of the tongue and other symptomatic behavior—all the little things we observe and describe when we present cases. From this the analyst tries to evolve a "conception" of what is "really" going on in the interaction and of what the person is "really" like at the intrapsychic core. In his clinical seminars, Bion (1987) gives many detailed examples of this process as he comments on various case presentations.

According to Bion, that conception "evolves" in the mind of the therapist on the basis of what is placed there by the patient's myriad communications. This Bion calls the "K." The next step is to give that conception, or "K," back to the patient such that the patient can use it to get acquainted with his or her "O." After that step, the therapist must help the patient to actually translate this new knowledge into change. Thus, intensive psychotherapy is a three-step procedure in which we first get an evolving knowledge ("K") of the "O" of that person by learning how to listen on all the channels. We then have to discover how to effectively communicate that knowledge ("K") back to the patient. Finally, we have to stand by the patient while the patient translates that knowledge into actual change by working it through in his or her daily life over and over again.

This is a very difficult craft to learn and practice and an even more difficult one to teach. The problem for the teacher is how to convey at least the first step—namely, how to listen. If one cannot listen to what the patient is saying, then one is halted before one begins.

For example, in a little book by Bion (1977), significantly titled *Attention and Interpretation*, he emphasizes the tension that exists in the minds of psychiatrists between their medical, empirical scientific training and the requirement that they actually listen to what the patient is trying to communicate. He writes:

> The analyst will soon find that he appears to be ignorant of knowledge which he has hitherto regarded as the hallmark of scrupulous medical responsibility. It is disconcerting to find that one is without an idea, say, that the patient has been married, or has children, or of certain events deemed by the analysand to have been of great significance. If the patient has paranoid trends and displays a tendency towards litigation it may seem to be running an unwarranted risk to be ignorant of matters that could, in a court of law, be regarded as significant and as evidence of ordinary medical care for detail. This would indeed be the case if there were not cogent reasons for *not* "remembering" such detail. As it is, I think that whatever the risks may be the obligation is for the analyst to conduct the case in accordance with his lights—and not in accordance with the supposed risks to himself. In this method the experience the analyst gains bears little resemblance to the files and case histories with which psychiatry is familiar. It may appear to differ from what would be

> expected in the light of accepted theory. Thus an analyst may feel, to take a common example, that his married patient is unmarried; if so, it means that psycho-analytically his patient *is* unmarried: the emotional reality and the reality based on the supposition of the marriage contract are discrepant. If this seems to suggest the analyst must preserve his capacity for memory, I maintain that he always does (as does the patient, however regressed), but error is more likely to arise through inability to *divest* oneself of memory than through forgetfulness. If the analyst does not remember that his patient is married, the fact that he *is* is irrelevant until the patient says something that reminds the analyst of this fact. [p. 49]

This is why in a course on listening it is best not to spend a great deal of time on reports of answers to the questions that constitute the classical type of psychiatric history as given in the usual case presentations in seminars. This is certainly not intended to mean that a student therapist should not learn how to present to a standard case seminar properly and to identify the DSM-IIIR syndromes. But like Bion, we must shake the student out of the customary approach because that standard approach will *interfere with* rather than enhance proper listening to a patient in intensive psychotherapy. The customary history is of course necessary for a diagnostic workup, a plan for somatic or pharmacological intervention, a formal case presentation, a court case, or a published case report. But in this very unique psychoanalytic situation, in which one is going to be in close contact with another person maybe two or three or even four times a week for several years, formal history-taking techniques may become a hindrance rather than a help. This is especially true if these techniques are extended beyond the standard diagnostic workup which most of us—correctly—feel obligated to undertake in the first few sessions for medicolegal reasons. Extensive and prolonged interrogation tends to prevail when therapists are anxious because they do not understand what the patient is trying to communicate, so question follows upon question. The therapist's notebook becomes filled with trivial detail that substitutes for the "K" that should be evolving, as illustrated in the cases discussed in Chapter 3.

Bion explains that although a patient responds to the usual history question by saying, "I am married; I have three children," we may recognize that the patient in the case Bion presents has to be listened to as if he were not married and has no children. Intrapsychically, he is an unmarried person. He is not relating to his spouse and children in the way we would want to relate to our spouses and children, or in the way we would assume that someone would ordinarily relate to a spouse and children. From the point of view of Bion's patient, his wife and children are either selfobjects (Kohut) or impediments or whatever else he uses them for; they may have no autonomous existence for him.

If the therapist cannot or will not place himself or herself into this patient's intrapsychic state, the therapist will make many errors in attempting to understand what the patient's complaints are really intended to communicate, why the patient is having problems in living, or even why the patient has come for treatment and what are the patient's expectations and early transference manifestations. Therefore the most common kind of generally accepted response to the standard question about marital status—"I am a married man with a wife and children"—cannot be listened to or accepted as it is in an ordinary psychiatric history; otherwise the patient will experience the therapist as just another person in a long line of individuals who had no real empathic understanding of him as a unique or "transcendent" individual. When the therapist repeats that pattern with the patient, the patient's autonomous self is ignored and recedes into the background; the patient as a "thing" or a "case" constitutes the foreground.

JOHN CAGE

Psychoanalysis is not alone in struggling with this unique problem of listening in order to develop depth understanding. A dramatic example of the same concentration on listening in depth comes from the thought and work of John Cage, a very unconventional composer. What Cage tries to do in a variety of ways is make the listener aware of those aspects of music, or aspects of a musical performance, that no one has paid attention to before. For example, he will have several works performed at the same time on the same stage. In other words, he takes the basic "background practice" of concert music, the basic, generally accepted structure that no one questions, and he questions and challenges it. This is in the tradition of continental philosophy from Heidegger to Foucault.

In another example, Cage was asked why it is that he offered three works that consist of total silence, three "musical" works. The following question was asked of Cage: If you have three musical works that consist of total silence, how do you differentiate among them? To illustrate his ideas, I have intermittently quoted from his (1976) book *For the Birds*, and I have interposed my explanations in brackets:

> "The first one [is entitled] *4'33"*. [In other words, it is four minutes and 33 seconds of silence. It] involved one or several musicians who made no sound. The second one [is called] *0'0"*. [Because it has infinite time, you can make it as long as you want. This]

> indicates that an obligation towards others must be fulfilled, in a partial or complete manner, by a single person. [In other words, on the stage there is someone fulfilling an obligation who has as long as he or she wants to take to fulfill the obligation in any way they wish to fulfill it.] The third one involves gathering together two or more people who are playing a game [with an amplifier present to amplify every sound of the game. For example,] a bridge or chess match, or any game at all can become a distinct . . . silent-musical work."
>
> Then the interviewer interpolated, "You said 'a distinct' work? That presupposes that the work already exists . . ."
>
> Cage replied, "Yes, in nature, and at every moment. 'Distinct' [only] means that there is amplification. [In other words, an amplifier on the stage picks up every sound as two people play chess or cards. These are sounds to which you would ordinarily pay no attention in your concentration on the game.] It's a work on a work—like all my indeterminate works! I say that it's essentially silent because I believe that it allows the silence of a game of chess to appear for what it really is: a silence full of noises!" [p. 210]

Cage draws attention to the fact that there is a *background* against which people present themselves, like the background against which a musical work is presented. Ordinarily, up to now, the background, the hall, the seated audience, the players, have been taken for granted, and the standard formal performance has been taken for granted. Cage now wants to bring that background into the foreground by a series of clever tricks. He wishes to call to our attention that the background does not have to be of a fixed nature. It can be changing and flexible, and it has a profound influence on the foreground!

For a similar example, during the 1983 American Psychiatric Association meeting in New York, I attended the London Symphony Orchestra's performance of Webern's *Six Pieces for Large Orchestra* at the magnificent Lincoln Center.

Although it was beautifully performed, the audience was clearly bored and began to cough; soon an epidemic of coughing broke out that was so loud that the musical performance could not be heard over it. The background at this point became the foreground—a concert of a cacophony of coughs!

In order to do intensive psychotherapy, one must understand that the generally assumed or taken-for-granted background has a profound influence on the foreground. The intrapsychic setting that the patient brings greatly influences both what the patient says and what he or she hears the therapist say, and therefore determines the effects of our interventions, no matter how accurate or well intended. This intrapsychic setting is constituted by the culture and interpersonal environment in which the patient developed, interacting in a complex and unique fashion with the patient's genetic predisposition, accrued intrapsychic representations, and compromise formations at each developmental stage. Thus the background for each therapist and patient will be different, and the dyadic process will be specific for that pair.

Our technical interventions, statements, and office ambience occasion the foreground, which falls on the patient's unique intrapsychic background, a background that cannot be taken for granted. If proper listening to the patient has not carefully established what that background is, then it is impossible to understand why the patient may respond so paradoxically to what appears to be a simple, intelligent, rational statement on the part of the therapist—for example, the apparently decent encouragement that any general practitioner or family physician would offer to a hypochondriacal patient, which only leads to more complaints. The patient's response simply makes no sense unless the therapist becomes aware of background aspects to which we ordinarily pay no attention in an interpersonal relationship. With this awareness, the response not only has meaning, but even more important, in opposition to those who devalue psychoanalysis as a science, it is quite predictable. With this knowledge of the background, such predictions no longer appear to be magic.

The teacher's most challenging problem—as in the example from Cage—is to jar the student out of assuming the background of the ordinary doctor–patient interaction, to call attention in every possible way to aspects of the relationship and aspects of the intrapsychic background of both participants that in ordinary relationships are not given attention, that are taken for granted except perhaps in cross-cultural exchanges. What makes this so difficult is that there is a tremendous resistance against facing these things, because whenever we are jarred out of the familiar and made to confront the unfamiliar or derivatives of the repressed, we become uncomfortable; we do not like it, and we do not particularly appreciate the person who calls our attention to it. Both Anton Webern—who suffered a breakdown and underwent "psychoanalysis" in 1912, living most of his life on the edge of starvation and obscurity—and John Cage were well aware of this! It was Nietzsche above all who discovered the importance of such taken-for-granted assumptions—he called them "illusions"—and he dramatically turned the attention of the Western world to them. For many years he was ignored and cast out from the academic establishment; even afterward, his works were long considered unsuitable reading for properly bred young people. As he himself said, "I am dynamite" (Chessick 1983b); he was a person who questioned the genesis and value of all commonly accepted "values."

CONTINENTAL PHILOSOPHY

Such an emphasis in psychotherapy happens to be quite consistent with the state of modern continental philosophy.

The whole movement in modern continental philosophy is against the assumed background in British and American academic philosophy, which has been trying unsuccessfully for some years now to make philosophy a "science." Most contemporary British and American philosophers have tried to present philosophy as a series of symbolic or logical maneuvers starting, for example, with the absolutely certain, such as "atomic facts," and then building on "self-evident" premises the way Euclid did or any science purports to do. Or, they tediously ruminate over the essential or precise meanings of words and propositions. The ultimate result of this Cartesian tradition has been to cut philosophy off from the important aspects of humanity and the important questions of life. Philosophy, as it is practiced today in many academic centers in the United States or in England, has largely become a sterile branch of mathematics. Most of it is of no interest to anyone except other specialists in mathematical logic. The journals published for these academic philosphers resemble those for technicians and scientific specialists, and they are unreadable to all but other initiates into their narrow field.

Continental philosophy, in its own ponderous and sometimes unnecessarily obscure way, has been trying to return to the essentials of human living—Heidegger calls them "ontological structures"—and to get humans back in touch with themselves and their possibilities. One of the ways that continental philosophy does this is through concentration on the hermeneutical study of background practices (Gadamer 1982). The hermeneutic alternative begins with Nietzsche's recognition that the "truths" of any culture are embedded in the background practices of that culture. These background practices ground the prevalent truths for that culture and determine accepted linguistic and practical meanings for that culture. If one is not aware of these omnipresent background practices, then one cannot understand why certain things that seem ridiculous to us are considered true by another person, especially from another culture. These background practices are *not* based on the empirical sciences; rather, they precede and underlie them in any culture, and they determine what passes for science in that culture; from them spring what Kuhn (1962) vaguely refers to as the prevailing paradigms for "normal science" in that culture.

For instance, Western empirical science is based on the assumption that the universe is regular and that laws can be found and given mathematical expression. There are no rational grounds for that assumption or, for example, for Einstein's deep conviction that "God does not play dice with the universe"—which wrongly caused him to reject quantum physics. Einstein's assumption is based on a cultural and even religious background practice that worked well as a ground for science up to his time, and it was even operative during his discovery of the theory of relativity. His inability to abandon his faith in it caused him to waste many long years of intellectual effort and to become isolated from modern physics.

An example from our own field of the human sciences shows the crucial importance of these background practices. When July 4th approaches, we hear on the radio a series of cautions: Please drive carefully because it is a holiday; drive carefully and reduce accidents; above all, do not drink when you drive; and so on. Then the broadcaster announces the by-now-familiar statistics: the National Safety Council is predicting X number of deaths on the highway, so drive carefully and then there will be fewer deaths. A crucial background practice is thus entirely ignored. The assumption is that the problem is to be dealt with in the same way that hallucinations or delusions are treated in organically oriented psychiatry: We treat the symptom—too many deaths on the highway. The treatment calls for encouraging people to drive more carefully: Approach them as rational beings; tell them that if they drive more carefully, there will surely be fewer deaths on the highway. If the patient cooperates and follows this prescription, then the symptom will be ameliorated—and certainly it is true!

What is the background practice? The background practice is embedded in a culture that encourages the use of the automobile to go across the street to visit a neighbor, and discourages the proper funding of public transportation so that one takes one's life in one's hands if one rides on the New York subway. Some time ago, to the horror of all civilized persons, a young and talented female flautist was pushed by a maniac in front of a New York subway train and lost a hand. There was no significant public outcry about this disaster, nothing was done, and it was soon forgotten. Our public transportation system is still dangerous and inefficient. Instead we clutter our highways and our cities with unnecessary automobiles, which, of course, statistically increases the chances of their bumping into one another and of people being killed. That irrational and maladaptive background practice is ignored, and we continue to poison the air with ever-increasing automobile exhaust fumes.

We do the same thing with our hallucinating and delusional patients when we administer drugs and say, "Now we are going to reduce your hallucinations and delusions by giving you drugs so that you can go back out into society and adapt to it—fit in to it and not be a problem to it." What is not being looked at in that situation is, How did that society produce you in the first place, and what can be done about it? And, How can we help you so that you do not have these hallucinations and delusions *and* at the same time do not have to adapt mindlessly to a society that does the damage? These issues seem not to be problems if one is practicing competent, everyday psychiatry, which calls for one to diagnose the patient, give the appropriate medication, maintain the patient in the hospital for the three insurance-reimbursable weeks, and then terminate the "treatment."

BACKGROUND PRACTICES IN PSYCHOTHERAPY

However, if one is practicing intensive psychotherapy and yet blindly complies with the background practices of a society that engages in harmful and destructive practices, then one is presenting the patient with a paradoxical communication and a duplicitous model. When intelligent and sensitive patients pick up this inconsistency, insurmountable problems result. They do not all catch on; psychiatrists who go along with this quasi-medical approach may have very busy practices indeed, because there are many patients who *want* collusion (Langs 1979). Those who want to go along with the therapist in a collusion or falsehood so that they do not have to face what they are really doing, or what is really going on, will not be good candidates for intensive psychotherapy unless we challenge the collusion right away.

It is *our* responsibility to pick up such areas of collusion. For this reason, one always should begin a supervisory case presentation by asking the student therapist, "How did the patient get to you? What was said to the patient in the beginning? What does the patient expect? Are you going along with those expectations?" If we start out by either implicitly or explicitly promising a collusion to the patient, uncovering therapy will never get off the ground, and we cannot expect that it will. It is what Bion pejoratively calls "lie therapy." And it is *our* doing.

Other branches of medicine pay little attention to these matters. They just take the common background for granted; they assume that the patient would prefer to be healthy; that pills bring relief, cure, and even happiness, as the media tells us over and over again; and so on in our deplorable cultural mainstream. One cannot ignore the common background in intensive psychotherapy, however, and sometimes it is also a mistake to do so in other specialties. The offices of many physicians in our society are filled with patients who are neither there for reasons of physical health nor intend to stop coming when a symptom is treated. They just produce another symptom and appear again, earning the label of "crock," a nuisance to the busy physician who has no time to listen; one's schedule is crowded with seriously ill medical patients, and listening skills are neither taught in medical school nor tested on examinations for medical licensure.

If students' cannot be jarred out of our blind cultural background and persist in treating humans as objects for scientific study, classification, and manipulation, they will never be able to understand each patient as a unique transcendental/empirical doublet (Foucault 1970), and will never be able to develop genuine empathy with patients or understand how our culture has formed them. If therapists cannot imagine themselves in the shoes of their patients and somehow give them the feeling that they really understand them intrapsychically—or, in the language of self psychology, empathize with their self states—and grasp what is emotionally important to them, then they cannot expect their patients to respond to them as someone who is potentially useful to them as a selfobject in resuming their development. Either there will develop a misalliance (Langs 1979) with a collusion, or the therapy will terminate or stalemate.

Therapists must show, by interpretations and other interventions, that they have properly listened and understand what troubles the patient, and they recognize how the world and human interactions appear from the patient's point of view. The therapist must be attuned to the affectual message behind each verbal communication. Compare the effect of interventions based on proper listening with the arrogant statement made by a "senior hospital physician" (Woollcott 1981) to a group of drug addicts that *he* finds it possible to get "high" from the beauties of nature alone. When one says that to a patient, what is communicated is, "I don't know anything about you. I just want to treat you as a thing. I say that to *all* my patients; I will back you up, help you, encourage you; I will be the coach." The patient does not have to have a unique individuality for us to say that. What we are indicating to the patient is that we are viewing him or her as somebody in a slot: Patient X with a chart and a number. That kind of all-too-common intervention destroys the patient's sense of the therapist's empathic competence and undermines confidence in the therapist's capacity to genuinely understand a unique human individual.

We are always dealing with human beings, and when they come for help, their difficulties are more than just symptoms to be treated. Their social, interpersonal, and unique intrapsychic concerns and cultural background practices constitute what all people have to live with, their being-in-the world. Take, for example, the threat of nuclear war, which certainly does, as a background, profoundly affect the way people think and live. Or what about the continuous exposure of our children to violence on television, so that the average child witnesses 13,000 deaths before the age of 15? If therapists are not somehow aware of these things, actively concerned with these matters in whatever ways and through whatever organizations they choose, then they do not understand the urgency of these matters and they cannot hope to understand where patients are coming from and what they are trying to communicate.

The crucial measure of a teacher's effectiveness is the ability to enable the student therapist to listen to people in a way that he or she has not listened to them before. This was Freud's fundamental impact on medical practice. The real expertise of the mental health professional is evident in a two-person relationship if he or she can actually hear what another person is trying to communicate at *all* levels: background practices (the phenomenological channel), intrapsychic preoccupations (the Freudian and the object relations channels), self states (the self-psychology channel), and interpersonal relations (the interactive channel). The therapist must also be able to perform the usual medical and scientific empirical diagnostic workup and must be thoroughly familiar with the use of psychopharmacologic agents, which are very important in the treatment of many conditions and have become an indispensable part of our therapeutic armamentarium.

THE DOUBLE NATURE OF HUMANS

A human is not a thing. Human potential and complexity is far greater than any "apparatus" and in principle (Foucault) can never be fully grasped. The human sciences can never be simply empirical sciences, and when they try to be, everything characteristically human is paradoxically lost. All effective intuitive intensive psychotherapists, regardless of their theoretical school or mode of listening, have been able to rise above the Cartesian notion of the human as just a scientific object.

Even Freud, although he spent much effort trying—not very successfully—to describe the human as a "mental apparatus," constantly had to fight with himself over his tendency to be transcendental, speculative, and imaginative. Finally he gave in to it in his later years, producing essentially philosophical writings about culture, religion, history, and other subjects; some (Gill 1978) would say that this shows even in his metapsychology. In reading various reports (Momigliano 1987) about how Freud actually treated his patients, it becomes obvious that he did not treat them as machines or "mental apparatuses" at all. When Lipton (1977a), in his study of Freud's actual work with Paul Lorenz (the Rat Man, discussed in Chapter 5) pointed this out, he started quite a controversy, because Freud took a humanistic stance toward patients for granted and did not formally write about his adherence to that stance. He just assumed that every physician would behave in this empathic fashion, producing what he called, in Gill's (1982) paraphrase, an "unobjectionable positive transference."

Indeed Gill (1982, 1988), with his focus on the therapist's contribution to transference formation, again calls our attention to the importance of an empathic ambience in psychotherapy, and Modell (1976) considers it a vital ingredient even to the therapeutic action of psychoanalysis. Inherent in Freud's early work was an effort to gain "respectability," and in his culture it was science above all that had respectability. But that is a background practice from his culture, and today it is falling into disrepute. The Nazi "scientists" who made the holocaust more efficient moved this question of the respectability of science from the background to the foreground, from where it can no longer be assumed to be true.

What Foucault tries to show, first using psychiatry as his example and then studying the other human sciences (even including general medicine), is that it is impossible to understand the human *only* as a physical-chemical apparatus. There is a difference between humans and all other objects of study, an unknown extra—the transcendental part. We can study a person as a physical-chemical machine in some branches of medicine, but when we actually intensively interact with that person and work with humans in what Foucault calls the human sciences—psychiatry, general medicine, social sciences, psychoanalysis, penology, economics, and the various humanities—we cannot reduce what we are doing to any empirical science without losing the essentially human aspects of the interaction (Chessick 1981).

Economists, for example, admit they cannot make a scientific or mathematical economic model that would predict the behavior of people, even in the simplest circumstances. Humans are always something more than can be described in studies that employ only pseudoquantitative terms. If our goal is to actually enter into the intrapsychic life of another person and understand that person, as this must be done in the human sciences, we cannot in principle accomplish it by a simple Skinnerian type of approach, a "black box" theory of mentation.

The model human science investigator I think Foucault has in mind is the novelist. A novelist can tell us something about a character that simply cannot be described in empirical scientific terminology. In fact, a really talented novelist such as Austen or Tolstoy or Joyce can make the reader live inside the character's mind. The skilled novelist does this so effectively that the character comes to life for the reader almost automatically, in a way that is different and more than could be enabled by any empirical description. Foucault's argument is that psychiatry and social sciences and economics can never be reduced to sciences like physics or biology. There is always going to be a transcendental uncertainty in those human sciences that cannot be reasoned away, no matter how hard we try. The attempt to reduce philosophy, humanities, medicine, sociology, psychiatry, and other human sciences to quasi-empirical sciences is intrinsically doomed to fail by the "doublet" nature of the subject.

The same is true of intensive psychotherapy. To conceive of patients simply as bearers of symptoms is feasible if one is primarily using somatic or pharmacotherapy, but in trying to enter into a person's life in order to make effective, lasting interventions, the understanding of the novelist is required, or the sensitive eye of the artist. Schwaber (1983c) points out that the scientific outlook for a long time obscured "the impact of the analyst-observer as *intrinsic* to the field of observation" (p. 386).

To the beginning supervisee, the supervisor's observations about a case sometimes seem to be magical, to be coming out of nowhere. Actually, they are (one hopes) the result of long years of careful and continuous self-training to see and to hear things that others do not. As we sharpen up our capacity to listen and observe over years of experience, and if we are willing and able to learn by our errors, interpretations that to the novice appear to be the result of intuition and magic actually arise from a sequence of very rapid, intelligible steps, which can then be explained to the student. Later, of course, we must also strictly discipline ourselves to look for validation by paying careful attention to the effects of our interventions.

LEARNING PSYCHOANALYTIC LISTENING

How does one learn to listen? Talented and dedicated instructors can help. Most important is one's personal psychoanalysis—to explore one's self as thoroughly as possible, and to continue to do so even after analysis, as beautifully reported in a very personal paper by Calder (1980). I have discussed the problems involved in self-analysis after one's psychoanalysis elsewhere (in press). Students also must obtain supervision on many cases so that, above all, when they stumble, the reason is discovered. To learn from our failures, we must do a careful psychological autopsy on every failed case (for examples, see Chessick 1971).

We all know from personal experience that if we sit with a person about whom we care and who is suffering, we can feel their suffering without having to elicit a list of symptoms. If we sit with a person who is tense and anxious, we can quickly and uncomfortably sense their tension and anxiety. There is something in us that registers without their having to give us a detailed description. Sullivan (1947, 1953) repeatedly emphasized the contagious quality of anxiety; in his footsteps, Pao (1979) focused on the unique—and diagnostic—interpersonal ambience produced by the schizophrenic. And if one is really skilled, one can quickly see through many symptoms that a patient presents—whether stilted speech or physical complaints or bravado or laughter or jokes—and sense the depression and suffering.

How do we sharpen that empathic instrument in our mind, that stethoscope, so that we can use such an approach to its greatest advantage? Immersing ourselves in the arts in order to "see" with the eye of the artist can help, as can carefully studying ourselves, studying our own mistakes, and taking classes, as well as carefully examining specific works of art that shake us up and make things appear different than they were seen or heard before. Perhaps it involves the shift from the left brain to the right brain, as Grotstein (1983) conceives of it. Those of us who are right-handed are trained to predominantly use the left brain, especially in medicine. In working with people, one has to be able to go quickly back and forth between cerebral hemispheres (although this is only a metaphor; the neurophysiology is not convincing). All great novelists do this and carry the reader along in the process, as Gardner (1983) elegantly describes their craft.

During case presentations, the student should actually experience the supervisor taking an analytic listening stance on all channels, in contrast to the empirical stance of the medical practitioner. Freud (1926) discusses this contradiction between the analytic and the medical-empirical listening stances at length in his lucid book *The Question of Lay Analysis*. The analytic listening stance is optimally suited for allowing the mind to evolve a concept ("K") of where that person is in their intrapsychic reality, in an effort to approach the "O" of that person. This is in contrast to the empirical-medical-deductive stance, which calls for us to actively ask questions, take a history, make interventions, perform measurements, and even put our hands on the patient in a physical examination. Both are valuable, but they are for different purposes and they interfere with each other. We cannot use both simultaneously because the employment of one stance will unavoidably skew the results received from the other. One must be able to shift back and forth as clinically indicated, depending on the treatment strategy and goals in each case.

EFFECT ON THE LIFE OF THE THERAPIST

Another task for the teacher is to communicate to students the importance and the excitement and the potential of the field. One might say to one's students, "Look around at various psychotherapists of your acquaintance, especially the middle-aged ones, and ask yourself, Which one of these therapists do I want to be like when I am 50? How is it that the ones who are *not* the way I want to be are the way they are? And how is it that the ones I *do* want to be like are that way?" For each student, this is a personal judgment. Indeed, one might say to all students, "Look around at your parents and relatives and friends and professors and politicians who are in their 50s. Ask yourself, Which ones do I want to be like? What kind of middle-aged man or middle-aged woman do I want to be like in 20, 25, or 30 years? *Now* is the time to look because when you are 55 years old, it is usually too late. Again, one must ask, "Why are they a certain way? What has kept them that way?"

A therapist in training is so busy just trying to learn all the diagnostic techniques, DSM-IIIR criterias, and pharmacological material that these considerations, which are actually philosophical, tend to get shuffled into the background, because they can wait. When they finish training and open an office, they are so busy trying to build a practice and pay their bills that such questions again tend to be put off. Time creeps along and the years pass imperceptibly. Most younger psychotherapists and trainees pay little attention to these matters, and papers such as McCarley's (1975) on the psychotherapist's search for self-renewal or English's (1976) on the emotional stress of psychotherapeutic practice are rare and superficial.

How many therapists have really thought about Greenson's (1974) "The Decline and Fall of the Fifty-Minute Hour"? Patients in their second or third treatment who have already been to psychiatrists, psychologists, social workers, and pastoral counselors teach us what kind of *person* the therapist was. We learn about what has happened to therapists who have stumbled into problems with patients—interminable stalemates, acting out, and all the other unfortunate and sometimes astonishing things that happen. I have even seen therapists take patients home to live permanently with them, along with their families. One must feel just as much compassion for the therapist at this point as for the patient.

Although we should completely comply with medical ethics about our responsibility to patients, and sympathize with the public's rage about therapists who are unethically entangled with their patients, we should also be aware of the problems with which the therapist must contend in the course of being in the field over 20 or 30 years. The practice of psychiatry and psychotherapy can be lonely and frustrating, and we must understand the especially deleterious effects of this, for example, as Murphy (1973) describes it, on therapists with narcissistic problems, and on the aging therapist with "narcissistic vulnerability." Psychotherapeutic work with the wives and children of psychiatrists (Chessick 1977c) teaches us how the family of the therapist can suffer, especially, for example, when the psychotherapist is what Bird, Martin, and Schuham (1983) call a "collapsible man of prominence." Student therapists must ask themselves, "What am I going to be doing with my patients in twenty-five years? What will my personal life be like?"

The quality of the psychotherapist's life, like that of the physician (Chessick 1969b), must be attended to as one might cultivate a garden or, as Santayana said, as one might produce a work of art. It requires a careful foundation, proper nourishment from the beginning, and continual attention to the very end. Besides the obvious importance of the quality of our lives for our own physical and mental health, this quality will also profoundly influence our work with patients—who can always be counted on to "catch on" to what we are like sooner or later—and will reflect itself in the health and happiness of those we love, and even in the community in which we are at home, the one, single family of humanity.

REFERENCES

Arlow, J. (1985). The concept of psychic reality and related problems. *Journal of the American Psychoanalytic Association* 33:521–535.

Atwood, G., and Stolorow, R. (1984). *Structures of Subjectivity: Explorations in Psychoanalytic Phenomenology*. Hillsdale, NJ: Analytic Press.

Bacon, F. (1620). *Novum Organum*. In *The English Philosophers From Bacon to Mill*, ed. E. Burtt, pp. 24–128. New York: Random House, 1939.

Basch, M. (1980). *Doing Psychotherapy*. New York: Basic Books.

_____ (1987). The interpersonal and the intrapsychic: conflict or harmony? *Contemporary Psychoanalysis* 23:367–414.

_____ (1988). *Understanding Psychotherapy: The Science Behind the Art*. New York: Basic Books.

Binswanger, L. (1958). The case of Ellen West. In *Existence: A New Dimension in Psychiatry and Psychology*, ed. R. May, E. Angel, and H. Ellenberger. New York: Basic Books.

——— (1963). *Being-in-the-World*. Trans. J. Needleman. New York: Basic Books.

Bion, W. (1963). *Elements of Psycho-Analysis*. New York: Basic Books.

——— (1967). *Second Thoughts: Selected Papers on Psycho-Analysis*. London: Heinemann.

——— (1977). Attention and interpretation. In *Seven Servants*, pp. 1–136. New York: Jason Aronson.

——— (1987). *Clinical Seminars and Four Papers*. Abingdon, England: Fleetwood Press.

Bird, H., Martin, P., and Schuham, A. (1983). The marriage of the "collapsible" man of prominence. *American Journal of Psychiatry* 140:290–295.

Black, M. (1987). The analyst's stance: transferential implications of technical orientation. *Annual of Psychoanalysis* 15:127–172.

Blum, H. (1983). The position and value of extratransference interpretation. *Journal of the American Psychoanalytic Association* 31:587–618.

Boss, M. (1963). *Psychoanalysis and Daseinanalysis*. Trans. L. Lefebre. New York: Basic Books.

Brandchaft, B., and Stolorow, R. (1984). The borderline concept: pathological character or iatrogenic myth? In *Empathy II*, ed. J. Lichtenberg, M. Bornstein, and L. Silver, pp. 333–370. Hillsdale, NJ: Analytic Press.

Brenner, C. (1982). *The Mind in Conflict*. New York: International Universities Press.

Bruch, H. (1973). *Eating Disorders*. New York: Basic Books.

——— (1974). *Learning Psychotherapy*. Cambridge, MA: Harvard University Press.

Cage, J. (1976). *For the Birds*. Boston: Marion Boyars.

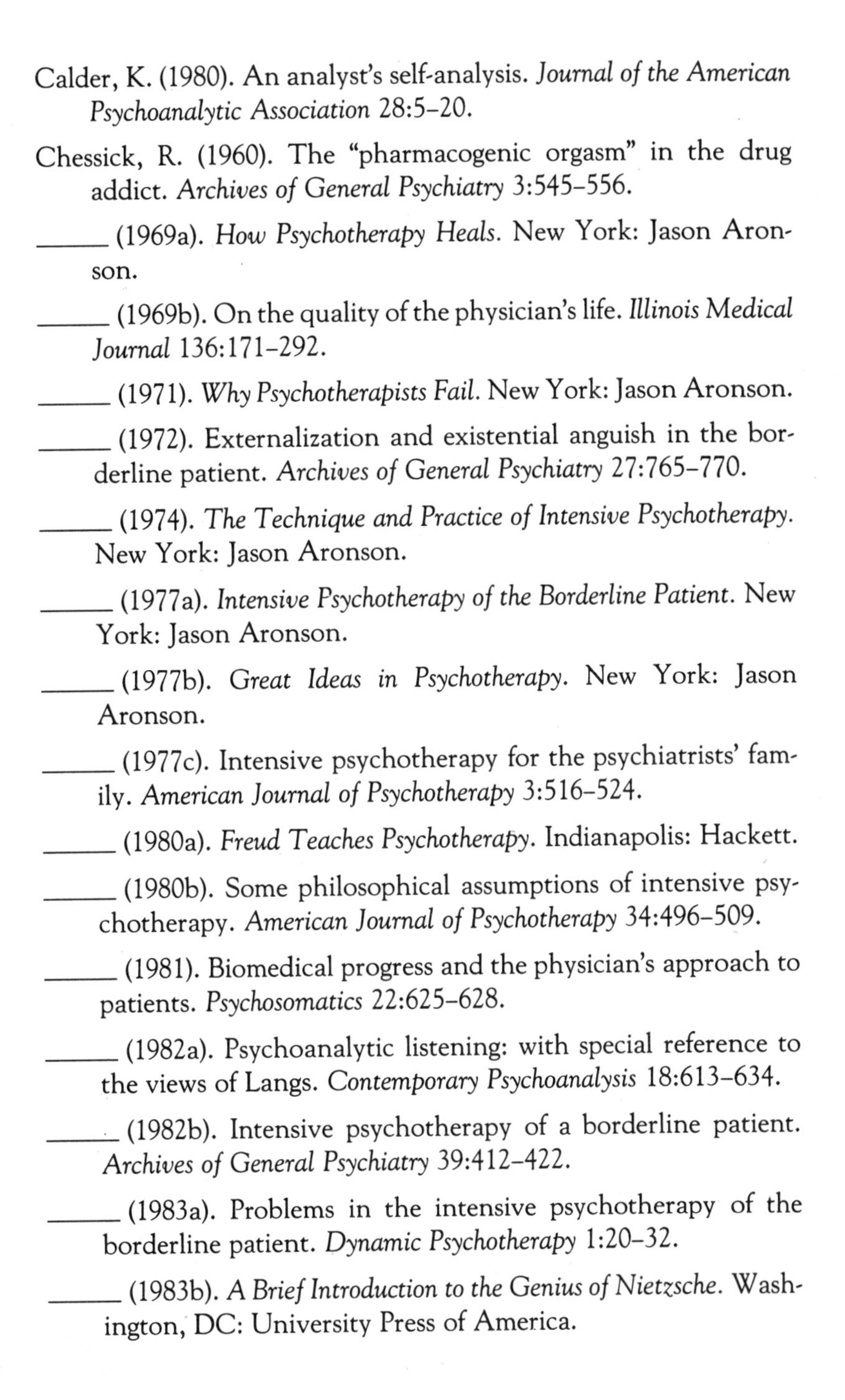

Calder, K. (1980). An analyst's self-analysis. *Journal of the American Psychoanalytic Association* 28:5–20.

Chessick, R. (1960). The "pharmacogenic orgasm" in the drug addict. *Archives of General Psychiatry* 3:545–556.

______ (1969a). *How Psychotherapy Heals*. New York: Jason Aronson.

______ (1969b). On the quality of the physician's life. *Illinois Medical Journal* 136:171–292.

______ (1971). *Why Psychotherapists Fail*. New York: Jason Aronson.

______ (1972). Externalization and existential anguish in the borderline patient. *Archives of General Psychiatry* 27:765–770.

______ (1974). *The Technique and Practice of Intensive Psychotherapy*. New York: Jason Aronson.

______ (1977a). *Intensive Psychotherapy of the Borderline Patient*. New York: Jason Aronson.

______ (1977b). *Great Ideas in Psychotherapy*. New York: Jason Aronson.

______ (1977c). Intensive psychotherapy for the psychiatrists' family. *American Journal of Psychotherapy* 3:516–524.

______ (1980a). *Freud Teaches Psychotherapy*. Indianapolis: Hackett.

______ (1980b). Some philosophical assumptions of intensive psychotherapy. *American Journal of Psychotherapy* 34:496–509.

______ (1981). Biomedical progress and the physician's approach to patients. *Psychosomatics* 22:625–628.

______ (1982a). Psychoanalytic listening: with special reference to the views of Langs. *Contemporary Psychoanalysis* 18:613–634.

______ (1982b). Intensive psychotherapy of a borderline patient. *Archives of General Psychiatry* 39:412–422.

______ (1983a). Problems in the intensive psychotherapy of the borderline patient. *Dynamic Psychotherapy* 1:20–32.

______ (1983b). *A Brief Introduction to the Genius of Nietzsche*. Washington, DC: University Press of America.

______ (1984). Sartre and Freud. *American Journal of Psychotherapy* 38:229–238.

______ (1985a). *Psychology of the Self and the Treatment of Narcissism.* Northvale, NJ: Jason Aronson.

______ (1985b). Clinical notes toward the understanding and intensive psychotherapy of adult eating disorders. *Annual of Psychoanalysis* 12/13:301–322.

______ (1986a). Heidegger for psychotherapists. *American Journal of Psychotherapy* 40:83–95.

______ (1986b). Transference and countertransference revisited. *Dynamic Psychotherapy* 4:14–33.

______ (1987a). Lacan's practice of psychoanalytic psychotherapy. *American Journal of Psychotherapy* 42:571–579.

______ (1987b). Kohut and the contemporary continental tradition: a comparison of Kohut with Lacan and Foucault. In *Frontiers of Dynamic Psychotherapy*, ed. P. Buirski, pp. 89–108. New York: Brunner/Mazel.

______ (1988). Prolegomena to the study of Ricoeur's *Freud and Philosophy*. *Psychoanalytic Review.* 75:299–318.

______ (in press). Self analysis: fool for a patient? *Psychoanalytic Review.*

Cooper, A. (1988). Our changing views of the therapeutic action of psychoanalysis: comparing Strachey and Loewald. *Psychoanalytic Quarterly* 57:15–27.

Curtis, H. (1985). Clinical perspectives on self psychology. *Psychoanalytic Quarterly* 54:339–378.

DeWald, P. (1987). *Learning Process in Psychoanalytic Supervision: Complexities and Challenges.* New York: International Universities Press.

Dreyfus, H., and Rabinow, P. (1982). *Michel Foucault: Beyond Structuralism and Hermeneutics.* Chicago: University of Chicago Press.

Edelson, M. (1984). *Hypothesis and Evidence in Psychoanalysis.* Chicago: University of Chicago Press.

Eigen, M. (1985). Toward Bion's starting point: between catastrophe and faith. *International Journal of Psycho-Analysis* 66:321–330.

English, O. (1976). The emotional stress of psychotherapeutic practice. *Journal of the American Academy of Psychoanalysis* 9:191–201.

Foucault, M. (1970). *The Order of Things*. New York: Vintage.

_____ (1973). *Madness and Civilization*. Trans. A. Smith. New York: Vintage.

_____ (1975). *Discipline and Punish*. Trans. A. Sheridan. New York: Vintage.

_____ (1980). *The History of Sexuality*. Vol. 1. Trans. R. Hurlog. New York: Vintage.

Freud, A. (1965). *Normality and Pathology in Childhood*. New York: International Universities Press.

Freud, S. (1901). *The psychopathology of everyday life*. *Standard Edition* 6:1–310.

_____ (1904). Freud's psycho-analytic procedure. *Standard Edition* 7:249–256.

_____ (1905). Fragment of an analysis of a case of hysteria. *Standard Edition* 7:3–124.

_____ (1909). Notes upon a case of obsessional neurosis. *Standard Edition* 10:153–319.

_____ (1911). Psycho-analytic notes on an autobiographical account of a case of paranoia (dementia paranoides). *Standard Edition* 12:3–84.

_____ (1912). Recommendations to physicians practicing psycho-analysis. *Standard Edition* 12:109–120.

_____ (1913). On beginning the treatment. *Standard Edition* 12:121–144.

_____ (1914a). Remembering, repeating, and working through. *Standard Edition* 12:145–156.

_____ (1914b). On narcissism: an introduction. *Standard Edition* 14:67–104.

_____ (1915). Observations on transference love. *Standard Edition* 12:157–171.

_____ (1917). Introductory lectures on psycho-analysis. *Standard Edition* 16:243–496.

_____ (1918a). The taboo of virginity. *Standard Edition* 11:193–208.

_____ (1918b). From the history of an infantile neurosis. *Standard Edition* 17:3–122.

_____ (1926). The question of lay analysis. *Standard Edition* 20:179–258.

_____ (1940). An outline of psycho-analysis. *Standard Edition* 23:141–208.

Fromm, E. (1941). *Escape From Freedom.* New York: Avon.

Gabbard, G. (1982). The exit line: heightened transference–countertransference manifestations at the end of the hour. *Journal of the American Psychoanalytic Association* 30:579–598.

Gadamer, H. (1982). *Truth and Method.* New York: Crossroad.

Gardner, J. (1983). *On Becoming a Novelist.* New York: Harper & Row.

Gedo, J. (1977). Notes on the psychoanalytic management of archaic transferences. *Journal of the American Psychoanalytic Association* 25:787–803.

_____ (1979). *Beyond Interpretation.* New York: International Universities Press.

_____ (1981). *Advances in Clinical Psychoanalysis.* New York: International Universities Press.

_____ (1984). *Psychoanalysis and Its Discontents.* New York: Guilford Press.

_____ (1986). *Conceptual Issues in Psychoanalysis.* Hillsdale, NJ: Analytic Press.

Gedo, J., and Goldberg, A. (1973). *Models of the Mind: A Psychoanalytic Theory.* Chicago: University of Chicago Press.

Gill, M. (1978). Metapsychology is irrelevant to psychoanalysis. In *The Human Mind Revisited*, ed. S. Smith, pp. 349–396. New York: International Universities Press.

_____ (1982). *Analysis of the Transference*. Vol. 1. New York: International Universities Press.

_____ (1988). Converting psychotherapy into psychoanalysis. *Contemporary Psychoanalysis* 24:262–274.

Gill, M., and Muslin, H. (1976). Early interpretation of transference. *Journal of the American Psychoanalytic Association* 34:779–795.

Giovacchini, P. (1975). *Psychoanalysis of Character Disorders*. New York: Jason Aronson.

Glover, E. (1956). *On the Early Development of Mind*. New York: International Universities Press.

Goldberg, A. (1987a). A self psychology perspective. *Psychoanalytic Inquiry* 7:181–188.

_____ (1987b). Psychoanalysis and negotiation. *Psychoanalytic Quarterly* 56:109–129.

_____ , ed. (1988). *Frontiers in Self Psychology*. Vol. 3. Hillsdale, NJ: Analytic Press.

Greenberg, J., and Mitchell, S. (1983). *Object Relations in Psychoanalytic Theory*. Cambridge, MA: Harvard University Press.

Greenson, R. (1974). The decline and fall of the fifty-minute hour. *Journal of the American Psychoanalytic Association* 22:785–791.

Grinberg, L. (1979). Countertransference and projective counteridentification. In *Countertransference: The Therapist's Contribution to the Therapeutic Situation*, ed. L. Epstein and A. Feiner, pp. 169–171. New York: Jason Aronson.

Grinberg, L., Sor., D., and de Bianchedi, E. (1977). *Introduction to the Work of Bion*. New York: Jason Aronson.

Grosskurth, P. (1986). *Melanie Klein: Her World and Her Work*. New York: Knopf.

Grotstein, J. (1983). Some perspectives on self psychology. In *The*

Future of Psychoanalysis, ed. A. Goldberg, pp. 165–202. New York: International Universities Press.

Gunther, M. (1976). The endangered self: a contribution to the understanding of narcissistic determinants of countertransference. *Annual of Psychoanalysis* 4:201–224.

——— (1984). The prototypical archaic transference crisis: critical encounters of the archaic kind. In *Psychoanalysis: The Vital Issues*, vol. II, ed. G. Pollock and J. Gedo, pp. 69–96. New York: International Universities Press.

Hegel, G. (1807). *Phenomenology of Spirit*. Trans. A. Miller. Oxford: Clarendon Press.

Heidegger, M. (1962). *Being and Time*. Trans. J. Macquarrie and E. Robinson. New York: Harper & Row.

Horney, K. (1987). *Final Lectures*. New York: W. W. Norton.

Hunt, W., and Issacharoff, A. (1977). Henrich Racker and countertransference theory. *Journal of the American Academy of Psychoanalysis* 5:95–106.

Husserl, E. (1913). *Ideas: General Introduction to Pure Phenomenology*. Trans. W. Gibson. New York: Macmillan.

Isaacs, S. (1939). Criteria for interpretation. *International Journal of Psycho-Analysis* 20:148–160.

Jaspers, K. (1954). *The Way to Wisdom*. Trans. R. Manheim. New Haven, CT: Yale University Press.

——— (1972). *General Psychopathology*. Trans. J. Hoenig and M. Hamilton. Chicago: University of Chicago Press.

Jones, E. (1953). *The Life and Work of Sigmund Freud*. Vol. 1. New York: Basic Books.

——— (1955). *The Life and Work of Sigmund Freud*. Vol. 2. New York: Basic Books.

Kahlbaum, K. (1973). *Catatonia*. Baltimore, MD: Johns Hopkins University Press.

Kant, E. (1781). *Critique of Pure Reason*. Trans. N. Smith. New York: St. Martins Press, 1965.

Kanzer, M. (1952). The transference neurosis of the Rat Man. *Psychoanalytic Quarterly* 21:181–189.

Kernberg, O. (1975). *Borderline Conditions and Pathological Narcissism.* New York: Jason Aronson.

_____ (1976). *Object Relations Theory and Clinical Psychoanalysis.* New York: Jason Aronson.

_____ (1980). *Internal World and External Reality.* New York: Jason Aronson.

_____ (1987). Projection and projective identification: developmental and clinical aspects. *Journal of the American Psychoanalytic Association* 35:795–819.

Klein, M. (1975). *Envy and Gratitude and Other Works 1946–1963.* New York: Delta Books.

Kohut, H. (1971). *The Analysis of the Self.* New York: International Universities Press.

_____ (1977). *The Restoration of the Self.* New York: International Universities Press.

_____ (1978). *The Search for the Self.* Ed. P. Ornstein. New York: International Universities Press.

_____ (1979). The two analyses of Mr. Z. *International Journal of Psycho-Analysis* 60:3–27.

_____ (1984). *How Does Analysis Cure?* Chicago: University of Chicago Press.

Kuhn, T. (1962). *The Structure of Scientific Revolutions.* Chicago: University of Chicago Press.

Kundera, M. (1986). *The Art of the Novel.* New York: Grove Press.

Laing, R. (1960). *The Divided Self.* New York: Pantheon.

_____ (1969). *The Politics of the Family.* New York: Vintage.

Langs, R. (1978). *The Listening Process.* New York: Jason Aronson.

_____ (1979). *The Therapeutic Environment.* New York: Jason Aronson.

——— (1982). *Psychotherapy: A Basic Text.* New York: Jason Aronson.

Lasch, C. (1978). *The Culture of Narcissism: American Life in an Age of Diminishing Expectations.* New York: W. W. Norton.

Lemaire, A. (1981). *Jacques Lacan.* London: Routledge and Kegan Paul.

Lichtenberg, J. (1983). *Psychoanalysis and Infant Research.* Hillsdale, NJ: Analytic Press.

Lipton, S. (1977a). The advantages of Freud's technique as shown in his analysis of the Rat Man. *International Journal of Psycho-Analysis* 58:255–274.

——— (1977b). Clinical observations on resistance to the transference. *International Journal of Psycho-Analysis* 58:463–472.

——— (1979). An addendum to "The Advantages of Freud's Technique as shown in his analysis of the Rat Man." *International Journal of Psycho-Analysis* 60:215–216.

——— (1983). A critique of so-called standard psychoanalytic technique. *Contemporary Psychoanalysis* 19:35–46.

Loewald, H. (1960). On the therapeutic action of psychoanalysis. *International Journal of Psycho-Analysis* 41:16–33.

——— (1986). Transference–countertransference. *Journal of the American Psychoanalytic Association* 34:275–288.

Malcolm, J. (1987). Reflections: *J'appele un chat un chat. The New Yorker,* April 29: 84–102.

McCarley, T. (1975). The psychotherapist's search for self-renewal. *American Journal of Psychiatry* 132:221–224.

Meyers, S. (1981). Panel report on the bipolar self. *Journal of the American Psychoanalytic Association* 29:143–160.

Meyerson, P. (1981). The nature of the transactions that occur in other than classical analysis. *International Review of Psycho-Analysis* 8:173–189.

Modell, A. (1976). "The holding environment" and the therapeutic action of psychoanalysis. *Journal of the American Psychoanalytic Association* 24:285–308.

Momigliano, L. (1987). A spell in Vienna: but was Freud a Freudian? *International Review of Psycho-Analysis* 14:373–389.

Money-Kryle, R. (1974). The Kleinian school. In *American Handbook of Psychiatry*, vol. 1, 2d ed., ed. S. Arieti, pp. 819–827. New York: Basic Books.

Murphy, W. (1973). Narcissistic problems in patients and therapists. *International Journal of Psychoanalytic Psychotherapy* 2:113–124.

Muslin, H. (1979). Transference in the Rat Man case: the transference in transition. *Journal of the American Psychoanalytic Association* 27:561–578.

Muslin, H., and Val, E. (1987). *The Psychotherapy of the Self.* New York: Brunner/Mazel.

Nietzsche, F. (1968). *Basic Writings.* Trans. W. Kaufmann. New York: Random House.

Offenkrantz, W., and Tobin, A. (1974). Psychoanalytic psychotherapy. *Archives of General Psychiatry* 30:593–606.

Ornstein, P. (1981). The bipolar self and the psychoanalytic treatment process: clinical-theoretical considerations. *Journal of the American Psychoanalytic Association* 29:353–376.

Ostow, M. (1979). Letter to the editor. *International Journal of Psycho-Analysis* 60:531–532.

Pao, P. (1979). *Schizophrenic Disorders.* New York: International Universities Press.

______ (1983). Therapeutic empathy and the treatment of schizophrenics. *Psychoanalytic Inquiry* 3:145–167.

Pieper, J. (1987). *Guide to Thomas Aquinas.* Notre Dame, IN: Notre Dame University Press.

Pine, F. (1985). *Developmental Theory and Clinical Process.* New Haven, CT: Yale University Press.

Quinn, S. (1987). *A Mind of Her Own: The Life of Karen Horney.* New York: Summit Books.

Racker, H. (1968). *Transference and Counter-Transference.* New York: International Universities Press.

Rangell, L. (1981). From insight to change. *Journal of the American Psychoanalytic Association* 29:119–142.

——— (1988). The future of psychoanalysis: the scientific crossroads. *Psychoanalytic Quarterly* 57:313–340.

Reed, G. (1987). Rules of clinical understanding in classical psychoanalysis and self psychology: a comparison. *Journal of the American Psychoanalytic Association* 35:421–446.

Reik, T. (1954). *Listening with the Third Ear: The Inner Experience of a Psychoanalyst.* New York: Farrar, Straus.

Ricoeur, P. (1970). *Freud and Philosophy: An Essay on Interpretation.* New Haven, CT: Yale University Press.

Roazen, P. (1969). *Brother Animal: The Story of Freud and Tausk.* New York: Knopf.

Rosen, J. (1953). *Direct Analysis.* New York: Grune & Stratton.

Shane, E. (1987). Varieties of psychoanalytic experience, 1. *Psychoanalytic Inquiry* 7:199–206.

Schneiderman, S. (1980). *Returning to Freud: Clinical Psychoanalysis in the School of Lacan.* New Haven, CT: Yale University Press.

Schwaber, E. (1981a). Empathy: a mode of analytic listening. *Psychoanalytic Inquiry* 1:357–392.

——— (1981b). Narcissism, self psychology, and the listening perspective. *Annual of Psychoanalysis* 9:115–131.

——— (1983a). A particular perspective on analytic listening. *Psychoanalytic Study of the Child* 38:519–546.

——— (1983b). Construction, reconstruction, and the mode of clinical attunement. In *The Future of Psychoanalysis,* ed. A. Goldberg, pp. 273–292. New York: International Universities Press.

_____ (1983c). Psychoanalytic listening and psychic reality. *International Review of Psycho–Analysis* 10:379–392.

_____ (1985). *The Transference in Psychotherapy: Clinical Management.* New York: International Universities Press.

_____ (1986). Reconstruction and perceptual experience: further thoughts on psychoanalytic listening. *Journal of the American Psychoanalytic Association* 34:911–932.

_____ (1987). Models of the mind and data-gathering in clinical work. *Psychoanalytic Inquiry* 7:261–276.

Segal, H. (1974). *Introduction to the Work of Melanie Klein.* New York: Basic Books.

Silverman, L. (1987). Discussion of paper by M. Black. *Annual of Psychoanalysis* 15:150–156.

Stern, D. (1985). *The Interpersonal World of the Infant.* New York: Basic Books.

Stone, L. (1961). *The Psychoanalytic Situation.* New York: International Universities Press.

_____ (1981). Notes on the noninterpretive elements in the psychoanalytic situation and process. *Journal of the American Psychoanalytic Association* 29:89–118.

Sullivan, H. (1947). *Conceptions of Modern Psychiatry.* Washington, DC: White Foundation.

_____ (1953). *The Interpersonal Theory of Psychiatry.* New York: W. W. Norton.

Thomä, H., and Kächele, H. (1985). *Psychoanalytic Practice 1: Principles.* Trans. M. Wilson and D. Roseveare. New York: Springer-Verlag.

Tolpin, P. (1983). A change in the self: the development and transformation of an idealizing transference. *International Journal of Psycho-Analysis* 64:461–483.

Tower, L. (1956). Countertransference. *Journal of the American Psychoanalytic Association* 4:224–255.

Waldinger, R. (1987). Intensive psychodynamic therapy with borderline patients: an overview. *American Journal of Psychiatry* 144:267–274.

Waldron, S. (1983). Review of Basch's *Doing Psychotherapy. Psychoanalytic Quarterly* 52:624–629.

Wilson, C., ed. (1983). *Fear of Being Fat.* New York: Jason Aronson.

Wolf, E. (1983). Concluding statement. In *The Future of Psychoanalysis*, ed. A. Goldberg, pp. 495–506. New York: International Universities Press.

——— (1985). The search for confirmation: technical aspects of mirroring. *Psychoanalytic Inquiry* 5:271–282.

Woollcott, P. (1981). Addiction: clinical and theoretical considerations. *Annual of Psychoanalysis* 9:189–204.

Zetzel, E. (1966). An obsessional neurotic: Freud's Rat Man. In *The Capacity for Emotional Growth*, pp. 216–228. New York: International Universities Press, 1970.

Zinberg, N. (1987). Elements of the private therapeutic interview. *American Journal of Psychiatry* 144:1527–1533.

INDEX